CALL ME ISHMAEL

Defying the Odds

by
Dartanyan T. Jamerson

Dedication

This book is dedicated to the memory of my mother Denise, my grandparents Lucius and Annie Beatrice Fleming, my biological grandparents, Willie Lee Jamerson, and my godfathers Bishop Odis A. Floyd and Richard Battle.

At my core, I am the man I am today because of these people and the deposit each of them made into my life. I could never adequately express the love that remains in my heart for them, the impact that they all had on my life, and the debt I owe to each of their legacies for standing me up in their own way, in this thing called life.

My Mother

She gets her own chapter and multiple mentions so I'll just say she was everything she could have possibly been for me. She was my mother, my protector, my disciplinarian, my music teacher, my guide, my sounding board, my counselor, my therapist, my cook, and my at-home Bible study instructor. The love I had, and still have, for her is unmatched.

My Grandparents

My mother's parents were 70 years of age when I was born so I grew up around great wisdom. Lucius and Annie Beatrice. She called him Honey and he called her Bunch. Yes really. They were the ultimate example of marriage and love! I learned a great deal from them that I still use today. My grandpa Lucius was one of the wisest men I've ever met. He helped instill in me the understanding that I should love my family but never let them kill my dreams; that I should do my best to keep my name clean, and he built in me the traits of a God-loving man. I never wanted to let him down. I wanted nothing more than to make him proud of me. He taught me to fish, to set a hook, drive a motor boat, drive a car, cut grass, hang drywall, mix and lay concrete, and so much more by the age of ten.

Most of all, he taught me about Jesus! He also taught me how to build my muscle memory. In fact, I would say that my ability to memorize and keep people's names after a short period of time is one of those that people like to talk about the most. I quote him often and still apply his wisdom to my life and my family. He went to be with the Lord when I was 14 and I still miss him today! He will always be my most valued and revered hero!

My grandma Annie was more loving than I can express. With only a 6th grade education from Allentown Pennsylvania, grandma could not spell my actual first name (Dartanyan). She opted to use my nickname (Darty) but could not spell it correctly either. Every birthday card until I was 10 years old read, "Dottie" and contained $5. She taught me to cook, clean, and sew at an early age. I tailor my own suits to this day because of the skill she taught me. I have many fond memories of grandma, but the most impactful are of the last memories we ever made. It was after she had been placed in a nursing home. The place was Chateau Garden's in Flint, MI. Long since closed but that was the place. Grandma had Alzheimer's and had become catatonic. She did not recognize my granddad, my little brother, or my mom. But she always perked up, smiled, and was hyper-responsive whenever mom brought me with her. Her eyes would get really big, she'd extend her hand for mine, and she would be alert the entire visit. She'd often shed a tear if visiting hours ended before she fell asleep. It was always easier to leave if she fell asleep first. She went to be with the Lord when I was 12 years old. Her funeral was the hardest thing I'd ever experienced in my young life up to that point. It was the first time I saw my grandfather cry. That totally broke me down.

Likewise, my biological father's parents showed me love in their own ways. Granddad wasn't a man of many words that I can quote here... LOL, but I remember him always giving me quarters to play the video game whenever I stopped in the dry cleaners. Grandma (Big Mama from here on) always made me feel welcome and there was nothing like staying the night at her house. It was an amazing feeling every time I stayed. So often, me and the other grandsons would be there, and we'd all spend the night.

Plus, she made the best Kool-Aid! I always felt love whenever I was there. Granddaddy passed away during my senior year of high school in 1991, and Big Mama passed away in May of 2014. I remember my name not being listed in either obituary as a grandchild. But then it would not have been, now would it?

Then there is Granddaddy Willie Lee Jamerson. He was such a great man, husband, father, brother, uncle, and grandfather! He always accepted me although he knew I was not biologically his grandson. He never treated me differently. He will forever be in my heart. I miss stopping by Baltimore Blvd to see and talk with him, and kissing him on the forehead as I ended our visit. I can still see him leaning in for that kiss. I'll love him forever!

My godfathers

Bishop Odis A. Floyd. So much I could say but so little space in this book. After my grandfather Lucius, as a little boy, he was who I saw lead his family. I am forever grateful to Momma Bren (Brenda Floyd) for sharing Pop with me. I also thank Tony, Leonard (keep enjoying Heaven bro!), and Nikki for sharing their father with me. Then, there was Richard Battle. The Maestro! What a gift he was to me! From the time I knew who I was, he was there. The way he cared for my mom and was a real friend and brother to her. And this dude could cook!!! Spaghetti anyone? I'll never forget all he was to me, and my brother.

Foreword

Pastor Deon Clark, Lead Pastor
Equation Church,
Greensboro, North Carolina

Dartanyan T. Jamerson, Overseer, Pastor, and Leader. The titles he holds and effortlessly balances are possible because of how he walks as a son, man, father, godfather, mentor, big brother and more than anything (to me) friend. In this book, Dartanyan walks through the pain of the deepest rejection a person can experience. At the same time, he shows us that we can and should have joy while processing life and all that comes with finding our place in the world.

He is quite transparent and uses his story to reveal the power of God at work. As you turn each page, you will see there is a great deal of humility in his reality! You will recognize relatable pieces of yourself as a child wrestling with anger and rejection, or just wanting answers. Walking through his timeline, you'll find his path and yours seeming to intersect as he deals with wins and unbearable losses. Beyond the openness of this work, Dartanyan is careful to show how God was there all along during his real-life issues, while making him into someone great!

In this book, you will see what it is to walk through heartache and come out victorious. You will see what it's like to forgive wounds that have been present and governing your life for decades. This is more than a story! "Call Me Ishmael" is an overcomer's manual! It is full of Godly wisdom that, if applied, over time will yield the fruit of righteousness.

As you read this book, it becomes obvious that just like his experiences, his name was ordained! Dartanyan, one who served a king faithfully and honorably!

Introduction

Most believers know the story. God told Abram (before his name was changed to Abraham) when he was 86 years old that he would have a son, and that He would make him the father of many nations, and establish a covenant with his seed and unto everlasting generations. So, everyone born in his bloodline would be a part of this covenant.

> [4] As for me, behold, my covenant is with thee, and thou shalt be a father of many nations. [5] Neither shall thy name any more be called Abram, but thy name shall be Abraham; for a father of many nations have I made thee.
> [6] And I will make thee exceeding fruitful, and I will make nations of thee, and kings shall come out of thee.
> [7] And I will establish my covenant between me and thee and thy seed after thee in their generations for an everlasting covenant, to be a God unto thee, and to thy seed after thee.
> **(Genesis 17:4-7, KJV)**

But Abram and Sarai (before her name was changed to Sarah) were impatient and in comes Hagar the Egyptian, her handmaid. Sarai presents Hagar to Abram to lie with and have a son because she was barren. Then Ishmael was born, but God still planned to keep His promise and told Abraham, he would yet have a son by Sarah.

> [17] Then Abraham fell upon his face, and laughed, and said in his heart, Shall a child be born unto him that is an hundred years old? and shall Sarah, that is ninety years old, bear? [18] And Abraham said unto God, O that Ishmael might live before thee! [19] And God said, Sarah thy wife shall bear thee a son indeed; and thou shalt call his name Isaac: and I will establish my covenant with him for an everlasting covenant, and with his seed after him.
> [20] And as for Ishmael, I have heard thee: Behold, I have blessed

him, and will make him fruitful, and will multiply him exceedingly; twelve princes shall he beget, and I will make him a great nation. **(Genesis 17:17-20, KJV)**

"Despite how Ishmael was conceived, the Lord kept his promise to both Abraham and to Hagar. In Genesis 21, God reassured Abraham that He would also make a nation of the descendants of Hagar's son "because he is your son, too" (verse 12-13). Today, we often focus on Isaac as he was fulfillment of God's promise in Genesis 15:4; but Ishmael was Abraham's too and Jeremiah 1:12 reminds us "God watches over His word to perform it." Ishmael was still a gift from God and so is Dartanyan T. Jamerson (Darty). His story is one of perseverance, redemption, and forgiveness. His humble beginnings and struggle with feelings of rejection were simply an opportunity for God to use his life as a testimony for others. Darty could've ended up anywhere, but God had other plans.

Throughout his life, the Lord has shown up time and time again and raised him up to be a man of God, a loving husband and father, and a mentor to so many. I consider it a privilege to have served as a witness of how God's faithfulness kept and sustained him during the difficult times and created opportunities and advancements for him simultaneously. Similar to the baby in Elizabeth's womb, my spirit leaped with joy when I learned that he was writing this book. I knew it would not only provide insight and healing for others, but be cathartic for him as well. As a beneficiary of the wisdom and revelation shared by Dartanyan, I am confident that this is only the beginning. His gift will continue to make room for him and allow all those in contact with him to be blessed."

Dr. Toyia K. Younger
god sister, Senior Vice President for Student Affairs –
Iowa State University

I am Ishmael. Not in the sense of being the firstborn, but from the perspective that I was not wanted and left to whatever the world was going to dish my mother and I. Verse 20 speaks to the fact that Abraham had cried to the Father on behalf of his son. I cannot say that my biological ever prayed to God for my well-being, but I can say God has always been with me. However, having never been claimed by my biological father my entire life, I often wondered what type of man I would become; what type of father would I be?

Know this, neither your upbringing, society, nor your children should dictate how you are to be a father. Your relationship with God does! It is His design and standard that sets the tone for our service as a father. Yes, service. **"Train up a child in the way he should go: and when he is old, he will not depart from it" (Proverbs 22:6, KJV)**. Providing your children with training, instruction, and guidance is a service. However, this job has a different compensation. The compensation for the service on this job is the level of honor and desire your children have for the Lord to be at the center of their lives, once they have come of age.

Of course, my perspective is that of a boy who would be a son, become a man, then a father, then a mentor, then a preacher, and then a husband. Did you catch that progression? If you missed it, go back two sentences and read it again. I recognized that this progression is exactly what happened to me over the course of my life. Likewise, so many other men have experienced this, and so many boys and young men are experiencing it as you read this. I also recognize there are many girls, young women, and more seasoned women, who have also experienced similar progressions during their lives, and much of or all of what I will share in this writing. May you all experience the healing God has for you and that you can have a productive relationship with a man or woman as God intended from the beginning. Then, I declare that the trauma you've experienced at the hands of boys who became men and fathers, or girls who became women and mothers, without being fathered or mothered, be healed through an encounter with the Lord.

My prayer is that this book speaks to the fatherless father and gives him encouragement and hope. You will read my story, and come to know how I was cast away but did not become a statistic. Moreover, you will come to know what God can and will do when you submit to His Will and purpose for your life. The writings herein will speak to some that have fathers in the home but have never had a fulfilling relationship. Likewise, it will undoubtedly speak to the boy in every man that had no choice but to figure out so much of life on his own. I pray that these writings bring conviction to fathers, who may read it in secret and admit their failures to themselves, change, and do better. It is so easy for any male to be a dad, but not all successfully become fathers.

This is my story. I do not mention any of the names that many may expect to see. It's not about them, it's about my life. The actual names of my biological grandparents and father are omitted intentionally as I have never desired to cause stress on the family in any way. Some might say my existence is enough stress within itself. Not to mention, I've never announced their names publicly to this point, so why start now? I've come through on the other side without too much loss, but I had to go <u>through</u> it. My late godfather, Bishop Odis. A. Floyd, used to say, "if you're going through, it means you're not stuck!" So, I say to you, keep moving. Don't get stuck.

My hope is that, as you read through this project, you find the courage to beat heartache and come out victorious. This is more than my story. In some ways, it's your story too. "Call Me Ishmael" is my overcomer's testimony! If you apply the Godly wisdom found here to your life, over time it will yield the fruit of righteousness in your life as well.

Know that whatever you have to overcome, can be defeated! May my story be the motivation you need to fight through with the power of Jesus Christ that resides within you.

[20] Now to Him who is able to [carry out His purpose and] do superabundantly more than all that we dare ask or think [infinitely beyond our greatest prayers, hopes, or dreams], according to His power that is at work within us, [21] to Him be the glory in the church and in Christ Jesus throughout all generations forever and ever. Amen.
(Ephesians 3:20-21, AMP)

Enjoy the following short stories. Everything you read will take place in the setting of my hometown of Flint, MI. I'm a proud Flintstone, born and raised there. As I walk you through my life, I'm confident that you will read something that resonates with your heart and spirit, that encourages you to seek God in all that you do, and find the healing you are searching for while also finding the courage to forgive what you think is unforgivable.

About the Author

My First Name

I was born Dartanyan Tymar Jamerson on October 25, 1973, to Denise Marie Fleming and my biological father in Flint, MI. I'll speak of him in chapter two. Mom named me Dartanyan, after the French Musketeer who served Louis XIV as captain of the Musketeers Guard. They were the royal guard for the king while he was outside of the royal residences. My mom was a Theater/Music major and The Three Musketeers by Alexandre Dumas was the first stage production they did. She loved the name and held on to it until I came along. Honestly, as a young boy I hated my name because it was so long, and because I didn't know what it meant. I would later learn its origin, and become familiar with the story of the Three Musketeers. Then, I read the books and my perspective changed all the more. D'Artagnan was an actual person. The story of the Three Musketeers was a fictional account of his life and the basis for the legend of his romantic escapades. Of course, the three main characters of the fictional story were Athos, Porthos, and Aramis, while D'Artagnan (full name: Charles deBatz de Castelmore d'Artagnan) was the fourth edition later in the story. These men too, were actual people.

My Middle Name

People always ask where my middle name came from. Before I was born, there were two men that were not my mom's biological brothers, but they were her protectors and her friends. Their names were Timothy Tuner and Arthur Ragsdale. Because of their relationship with my mother, she combined their first names and created my middle name. So, Timothy and Arthur were combined to create Tymar (Tim-Are). Uncle Tim passed away in 2019 almost a year after mom, and uncle Arthur resides in Flint, MI and he and I remain in contact and good relationship. I love him greatly. God has done some amazing things in his life. I'm proud of him. He'll be getting married soon. Congrats Unc.

My Last Name

I was born into a situation that did not hold success as a certain outcome. My surname Jamerson is that of the man my mother married with him having full knowledge that I was not his biological son. They would then have a son together, my baby brother Willie Joe Jamerson, Jr. (Jay Jay). He and I grew up close, and remain close to this day. The knowledge that we do not share the same father is something we've known since the ages of 7 and 5, but did not fully understand until our teen years.

The existence of my two older brothers never became an issue between Jay Jay and I as there has never been an acknowledged connection between me and them. He always hated that I wasn't acknowledged and resented that my biological was a man of the church yet denied me as his son. I am thankful for Jay Jay's father stepping up and stepping in where he was not obligated; for giving me the last name I carry, and for owning me as a son. Nonetheless, the Jamerson bloodline is mine even though I wasn't born into it. I carry the name and have always honored it. I will continue to honor it until my last breath.

> "Every man-child needs a name. He needs an identity. He can't get that from his mother. Mothers are capable of giving great love and encouragement to their sons, but they cannot give them their identity. Only a father can do that" (Jakes, 1997).

By now, you may have a lot of questions bouncing around in your head. Just keep reading.

My Village and My Gift

With the help of her parents, my great grandmother MaDea, The Floyd, Younger, Montgomery, Bell, Brown, Simpson, Broadway, Nelson, Rhymes, Blassingame, Ross, Jarrett, W. Hill, R. Hill, Moore, Mills, Bailey, Dixon, O. Harris, B. Harris, LaValley, Chilton, Hightower, Williams, Johnson, B. Jackson, Battle, Carter, and Hopewell families, my mother set me on my life's path. Yeah, those families were and still are my village! Their love and support have been my strength and energy my whole life.

Mom's love for people and gift of music rubbed off on me early. I began to beat on drums at the age of three, but began to actually play the drums at the age of seven. I will never forget that night at the New Jerusalem Baptist Church Inspirational Voices (IV's) rehearsal when no drummers were there and I courageously climbed up on the drums and fell in the pocket and groove of the song best I could for a 7-year-old. From that day on, I was confident I could use my gift for God. Over the years, I polished my skills and was blessed to play drums on two live recordings, and two studio recording projects. I was humbled to accompany some of the all-time greats in Gospel music over the years. Most memorable of were, of course, playing for my late mother and late godfathers Bishop Floyd and Richard Battle. Others include: The Voices of Metropolitan, New Experience Singers, Elder A. J. LaValley, Bishop Paul S. Morton, Sr., Bishop James Morton, William Murphy III, New Jerusalem Full Gospel Baptist Church Inspirational Voices, Odelia Dunlap and the Northwest Community Gospel Choir, Veshawn Mitchell, Byron Cage, Bishop Larry D. Trotter, Ben Tankard, Dorothy Norwood, Dorothy Bloat, Ricky Dillard, Derrick Milan, Nuana Dunlap (Aunt NuNu) to name some.

I may not have been the best drummer, but I was always faithful and worked hard at my craft. I wanted to please God with my gift, so I always gave my best.

My Calling, My Request

In my late teenage years, I discovered a love for children and youth ministry. Being able to connect with them on multiple levels due to my own life's experiences seemed to make me a natural. I would later come to understand the anointing that God had placed on my life to do ministry. It was so much more than just something I would enjoy. It would become a passion, and what I would recognize to be my calling.

Holy Spirit called me to preach while I was sitting on the drums at Church one night. I heard Him but ran from it for nearly 10 years. Then I had my Gideon moment. I was ready to accept my calling, but needed to have a discussion with God, and get a response first.

> ^{36} And Gideon said unto God, If thou wilt save Israel by mine hand, as thou hast said,
> "^{37} Behold, I will put a fleece of wool in the floor; and if the dew be on the fleece only, and it be dry upon all the earth beside, then shall I know that thou wilt save Israel by mine hand, as thou hast said. ^{38} And it was so: for he rose up early on the morrow, and thrust the fleece together, and wringed the dew out of the fleece, a bowl full of water.
> ^{39} And Gideon said unto God, Let not thine anger be hot against me, and I will speak but this once: let me prove, I pray thee, but this once with the fleece; let it now be dry only upon the fleece, and upon all the ground let there be dew. ^{40} And God did so that night: for it was dry upon the fleece only, and there was dew on all the ground."
> **(Judges 6:36-40, KJV)**

My experience was not so different than this, except I only asked Him to prove it was Him, once. My conversation and request went exactly like this: "Lord I'm sure this is you, but I have one request. If this is truly you, I need you to send someone to me to tell me just the way I just asked you." What was unique about this prayer is that I prayed it inaudibly. I was in a room alone, and I spoke no words, so that only God could hear and know this request. I needed to see Him act upon my request. It would solidify my complete surrender to this calling. I'm sure only Gideon and I have ever needed God to show us in a direct and undeniable way in order for us to embrace His directives.

Then it happened. On a Wednesday night, during intercessory prayer in the chapel, Elder Brenda Echols-Smith walked up to me and my life was forever changed. She looked up at me right in the eyes and said, "Preacher, it's time! The Lord told me to tell you, you've been waiting on Him to send someone to tell you that you're supposed to preach the Gospel, so here I am to tell you." I fell to my knees and wept! I accepted my call to the ministry that night. I'll never forget all that led up to that moment that night. Since then, I haven't been perfect, but I've been as faithful as I could be in this flesh. But then, He always knew the man He was calling to do His work.

> "[75] I know, O Lord, that thy judgments are right, and that thou in faithfulness hast afflicted me. [76] Let, I pray thee, thy merciful kindness be for my comfort, according to thy word unto thy servant. [77] Let thy tender mercies come unto me, that I may live: for thy law is my delight."
> **(Psalm 119:75-77, KJV)**

My Development

After I'd been appointed as the State of Michigan Children & Youth Director for the Full Gospel Baptist Church Fellowship International, my mother told me stories of how my godfather (Bishop Floyd) had led the Great Lakes Baptist Youth Department when he was Reverend Floyd, and he was elevated up to and through to the National Baptist Convention. That was something I had no idea about, but it was how so many of them that attended the church knew him. Of course, there were thousands that followed him across the community and country because of his radio broadcast, his singing and music ministry, his huge personality that matched his huge physical make up, and his powerful exegetical and culturally relevant preaching style. Moreover, he was also an amazing person.

I would travel to accompany Bishop when he was in revival or for preaching engagements, along with my favorite Minister of Music (after my mom), Elder Allison J. LaValley (Jeff). Bishop would always leave me encouraged and challenged at the same time. I promise he could preach about the Children of Israel wandering in the wilderness for 40 years and my feet would hurt a little after the way he would bring the text to life! My favorite sermon opening of his ever, is, "As the curtain rises on the scene of this text." Man, he could work a text! However, my most favorite moments outside of being at the house with him and Momma Bren, or hearing him on Sunday morning, were attending Tuesday night Bible Study! O…M…G!! Listening to him teach and preach gave me life!

My Bishop (I called him Pop in Private.)

I have so many memories of Bishop Floyd that are mine alone. However, there is one that I will share here as it speaks to the man, mentor, father figure, and Pastor he was to me. I was his barber for years. I started cutting his hair right before he decided to go bald. Giving him a fade with that gray hair was one of the coolest things for me. Then the bald cut and shave was always fun too. He would turn his head ever so lightly to assist me as I cut his hair. He did this because I would always cut his hair at the house or in his office at the church, so there was no barber chair to spin, lol.

One day Pop calls my name. He said, "Darty (like only he could), go to my top drawer on my desk. Open it up. That's yours." Well, it was like $220. He asked, "why you keep leaving your money? You ain't gonna block my blessing." I laughed because that's when I discovered he had been leaving $20 on the counter or next to my clippers but I never picked it up because he hadn't told me it was mine. So he would put it back in his pocket until the next time. That went on for about 2 months or so and then he sent me to his desk after a cut.

The moral of the story here is, I'd never planned to charge him for a haircut. He was my dad, my mentor, my leader, and I was honored to care for him in that way. My blessings were being stored up with the Father because I was serving His man in the earth! But Pop wanted to bless me, so he did. I could not have started cultivating my ministry under a better mentor. I can truly say I have experienced some of the same Grace that was on His life. To him, I am forever grateful!

If you serve, serve with your whole heart. I believe there is such an anemic pool of true servants today. I watch people serve with such selfish and ulterior motives today. I'm glad I learned the right posture of serving at a young age. I learned to be seen and heard only when engaged while serving, but then also to be present without being a distraction. Speak when spoken to, and how to hear without listening.

Translation: servants are in rooms of great importance and have access to discussions of private content. It is never acceptable to retain what you hear for your own use. That has been lost on many of today's servants. Selah.

"[41]He that receiveth a prophet in the name of a prophet shall receive a prophet's reward; and he that receiveth a righteous man in the name of a righteous man shall receive a righteous man's reward. [42] And whosoever shall give to drink unto one of these little ones a cup of cold water only in the name of a disciple, verily I say unto you, he shall in no wise lose his reward."
(Matthew 10:41-42, KJV)

Table of Contents

Dedication iii

Foreword vii

Introduction ix

About the Author xv

Chapters:

Chapter One 01
My Momma

Chapter Two 13
Call Me Ishmael

Chapter Three 21
The Son

Chapter Four 29
The Man

Chapters continued:

Chapter Five   35
The Father

Chapter Six   49
The Mentor

Chapter Seven   61
Defying the Odds

Epilogue:

Thank You   69

References   75

CALL ME ISHMAEL

Defying the Odds

by
Dartanyan T. Jamerson

Chapter 1

My Momma

"[28]Her children rise up and call her blessed; her husband also, and he praises her: [29]Many women have done excellently, but you surpass them all."
(Proverbs 31:28–29)

Born For Greatness

My mother, Denise Marie Fleming was born May 8, 1955 in Detroit, MI and adopted eight days later by Lucius and Annie Beatrice Fleming. She was raised in Flint, MI. Initially, they lived down in the Saint Johns area. Then to 722 E. Lomita Ave. in the home her father built by hand along with his brother, my great-uncle Quincy. My grandparents loved her greatly and afforded her everything a child could need, want, and even dream of. The stories they would tell me about her were exciting and helped me learn who my mother was even better than I already knew her. My mom was often referred to as the "spoiled little rich girl" because she was an only child, always had a nice car, nice clothes, and didn't seem to want for anything. They reared my mom to trust and fear the Lord. She accepted Jesus Christ as her personal savior and was baptized at the age of seven at the Metropolitan Missionary Baptist Tabernacle.

My mom was phenomenal from a young age! She showed great promise in the music and arts arena from the time she first sat down to a piano. My mom was a child prodigy; attending the Interlochen Center for the Arts each summer for eight consecutive years as a child. She was a star pupil of the late great Addie Mae Simpson where she studied and mastered the art of music composition, choir accompaniment, and direction. In fact, she was treated like one of her own children. Almost immediately her anointing and gifts began to take form.

She began playing the piano and directing choirs at the age of eight. She would stand up on the director's box (traditional Baptist Church folk know about this box-LOL) where she would direct and sing. Mom attended Jefferson Elementary, Bryant Middle School, and was a proud graduate of Flint Northwestern High School (Home of the Wildcats) in 1973. She was proud to be a product of Flint, MI.

My Mom's musical career and legacy spans across six (6) generations. As a musician at Metropolitan Missionary Baptist Tabernacle, mom served as musician and directress for: the Blue Bells, (who would become the Voices of Metropolitan), the Gospel Chorus, Senior Choir, and the Youth Choir. The Voices of Metropolitan and the Youth Choir were known throughout the city for their powerful and anointed singing. My mom went on to impact music ministries across the city of Flint, Detroit, and across the state of Michigan, and later Erie and Meadville, PA, as well as Savannah, GA. Mom's gift impacted the following ministries: The New Jerusalem Full Gospel Baptist Church, Mt. Zion Missionary Baptist Church, Antioch Missionary Baptist Church, Christ Fellowship Missionary Baptist Church, Ebenezer Ministries, Shiloh Missionary Baptist Church, Canaan Baptist Church, Gethsemane Baptist Church, Detroit Street Church of God, First Union Baptist Church, Macedonia Missionary Baptist Church, Mt. Nebo Baptist Church, Mt. Olive Missionary Baptist Church, King Solomon Baptist Church, St. Paul Missionary Baptist Church, Foss Avenue Missionary Baptist Church, Vernon Chapel AME Church, Eliezier Church-of the Apostolic Faith, Greater Holy Temple Church of God in Christ, Thankful Missionary Baptist Church, Living Hope Community Church, Mt. Moriah Missionary Baptist Church, and the Mt. Pisgah Missionary Baptist Church.

Mom also impacted the Flint Community School District through her work with the Chapter One (Title One) Children's Choir that performed music by some all-time greats like Stephanie Mills and Kenny Rodgers. They also made appearances at the Michigan State Capital in Lansing, MI where they sang in the State Rotunda. My mom was not only a singer but also a songwriter; penning the popular song (He Giveth More Grace) recorded by the late great Reverend James Cleveland. My mom worked with some of the greatest in gospel music during her lifetime like Bishop Odis A. Floyd, Allison Jeffrey LaValley, Andre Crouch, Edwin and Tremaine Hawkins, Richard Smallwood, Mattie Moss Clark, Reverend Charles Nicks, Dorothy Bloat, Kurt Karr, and Dorothy Norwood.

Lifestyle Choice

Mom's life was far from perfect, and she never professed it to be. She experienced a great deal of hurt. She experienced so much hurt from those she was supposed to be able to trust, from those who said they loved her, and from those who were supposed to lead her, it eventually drove her to a dark place in life. That dark place manifested in the form of lesbianism and a crack addiction. So, from the time I was in the 3rd grade I had an auntie! Meaning my mom slept in a bed with a woman and not a man. We lived in a three-bedroom home. I didn't understand at first why they shared a room since there was an empty room and Jay Jay and I shared one room For years I was clueless. Then my neighborhood friends started saying really bad things about my mom and "our auntie". Then reality set in. That was when I recognized that she could not possibly be our aunt! So from the 3rd grade until my freshman year of college, my mother chose to live a lesbian lifestyle.

I say chose because it is not a disease or genetic irregularity as many would suggest. It's a choice! A choice she made because it was a safe place for her to retreat from her trauma. Safe from the trauma and the hurt of men, from the hurt of lying womanizing deacons, pastors, and other church leaders, and the hurt of judgmental people. So she thought. She experienced lots of ridicule and judgment from many people because of her chosen lifestyle. However, my grandparents continued to love her unconditionally although they did not condone her lifestyle choice.

After both grandma and grandpa died, I continued to formulate my beliefs on how my mom lived; the lifestyle choice that she preferred. I asked her about it, and she was embarrassed. She vehemently set me straight! She told me,

> "Dart, this is not how God would have any of us to live. He loves us, but this is not pleasing in His eyes. I'm going to get my life right. I promise. My prayer is that God protect you and Jay from this life! I don't know what I would do if this lifestyle were to touch the two of you"

I know for a fact that one of the things she was most pleased about, was that the homosexual spirit and lifestyle did not attach to either of us. However, in all of my growing and becoming, my mother's lifestyle choice actually helped shape how I would love unconditionally throughout my life. Subsequently, I formulated my LOVE philosophy based on the highs and lows resulting from mom's lifestyle choice. What is this LOVE philosophy you ask? Here it is:

L.O.V.E.
- o **L**isten
- o **O**pen Your Heart to Understand
- o **V**alue all of God's Word
- o **E**ncourage others to do the same

You should always try to LOVE first. Your actions could make the difference between someone meeting Christ or determining that they don't want to know Christ at all.

> "I like your Christ, I do not like your Christians. Your Christians are so unlike your Christ"
> -Mahatma Gandhi

Far too many people are professing Jesus, but in no real way are they reflecting or resembling Him. Love is a fundamental attribute every true follower of Jesus must express and live by.

> "By this shall all men know that ye are my disciples, if ye have love one to another" **(John 13:35, KJV)**

A Close Call

Because of hurts I've mentioned, failed relationships, disappointments, and also feeling like she had missed the mark and let her parents down, my mother would also become a functioning crack addict. One day, the ice cream truck was coming down our street and like normal mom would let my little brother and I rummage through her purses in her closet looking for loose change. Jay Jay happened upon a white hard piece of what looked like candy to him. He presents it to mom and asks, "mom can I have this candy?" The look on mom's face was terrifying and I knew something was wrong. She quickly took it from his hand, gave us both change for ice cream and sent us out to the truck. Later she would tell me that what he found wasn't candy, but a piece of crack cocaine and how it could have killed him had he eaten it. She sat with me in the living room and cried for most of the afternoon into the early evening. Remember, I told you I was her confidant. I cried with her because I could see how bad she felt. I was so glad my baby brother didn't eat what he thought was candy.

The Cost of Addiction and Her Turning Point

Mom would conduct several rehearsals throughout the week. Then, she would play and sing for those same churches on a Sunday morning because she had such an amazing gift and skillset. All the while being high or itching to get to that next high. She was a highly functional addict. However, no one knew. Although she lost weight, the weight loss looked natural and no one outside of her circle really knew what was going on. She remained flawlessly beautiful!

Sadly, once my Grandpa Lucius passed away, mom's addiction would cost our family greatly. Grandpa Lucius had created a respectable amount of what would have been generational wealth. Yet, my mother's addiction would cause her to squander more than $137K in liquid assets, three (3) houses, a summer cottage in Idlewild, MI, one (1) car, one (1) Motor home, and three (3) boats. In all, mom's addiction would cause her to go through upwards of $430K in cash and assets. When it was all said and done, there was great shame added to the lifestyle and addiction that had consumed mom for so many years. It would take many years before Jay Jay could forgive her for losing everything. He always felt that we should have had a better start into adulthood with what our grandfather had built to hand down to us.

The realization of these series of events was mom's turning point away from crack cocaine! She successfully kicked the drug addiction. She turned from crack cocaine and never went back. She was proud of herself and I think I was even more proud of her. The one place she struggled most was in fully forgiving herself for squandering all grandpa Lucius had left us. That was a tough place. But I never let her feel like I held bitterness toward her because what she had lost.

Jay Jay on the other hand wasn't as accommodating as me. He was very angry that the houses and the money were all gone. The difference between he and I was that I felt more like the adult in the conversation. I understood what had actually happened in a much better way than he did. I felt like I walked through it with mom, whereas he only saw it from the perspective of a child. It scarred him in a great way. It scarred me as well, but mine was suppressed and would not surface until many years later in my adulthood. But God is so real! He has always been real in our lives. Even when mom's actions did not align with His will for her life.

Mom Took Us "Down to The Set"

There came a point where Jay and I were exposed to drugs (cocaine, crack, marijuana, syrup, pills) and alcohol to a degree that mom must have gotten scared that we would not be able to avoid its grasp. So, Mom took us on a field trip that will probably cause some who read this to cringe. It was 1983. I was 10 and Jay was 8 and mom decided to take us down to "The Set." The Set was a place located on Detroit, Street (about a half mile from downtown Flint, MI) where drug addicts, drug dealers, pimps, and prostitutes hung out and did their business. On "The Set" there was a three-story brown home where people bought and used drugs. You could pull right up and buy anything you wanted. A man my mom knew named Isaac came to the car and put his hands on the door where the window was down. Mom made Jay and I sit up from the back seat to look at his hands and arms. We could see the holes from the many heroin injections. I was so afraid but I couldn't let my little brother see it on my face. I just looked and listened to my mom explain what we were looking at. As I reflect on this moment in my childhood, I'm torn between being amazed that she took us to see that and the fact that her friend allowed himself to be our show and tell lesson. I'll never forget Isaac.

That lesson and those images are some I will never forget. It's like it was a movie scene. However, it was real life and something that I'm grateful I experienced. Long before 2 Chainz every said it, my mom was "different". The three-story brown home is no longer there, but the same three churches that were there then, are still open today. I know people say that addicts have to want to change, but I'm angry that the church (3 individual churches in fact) was within a block of this place and no real impact was ever made. This house being gone was due to now actions of the area churches. The Church seems to choose what it wants to be vocal about. I'm not advocating for the Church to take on every societal issue, but I believe that we the Church must be angry about what angers God. Our hearts must break when we encounter what breaks God's heart. If we take this position, I believe He will always give us the strength and wisdom we need to be able to be His voice and His hands and feet in the earth.

Deliverance and Restoration

Mom decided that enough was enough. She was no longer going to be held hostage by the guilt and shame of having lived the lifestyle she lived, and for losing what amounted to a great head start to life for both Jay and I. She decided she was going to forgive herself and to let Jay deal with it however he felt he needed to. She was not going to be an enabler to him any longer. This was extremely hard for mom. After all, he was her baby boy and although she did not worry about me, she absolutely worried about him. She and I continued to discuss things on a regular basis as we did when I was young. We would still communicate about nearly everything. However, our conversations were now about how God was working in her life. How He had rid her of the desire connected to her addiction and ultimately her lifestyle choice. She no longer had a taste for crack cocaine, thus her addiction was gone! Also, He removed all unnatural desires for lesbian encounters. They were no longer present! What a mighty God we serve! He did that for my mom. Perhaps you are reading this and can think of someone you know that could stand to be encouraged at the availability of such deliverance. Perhaps their issues are the same, or slightly similar, but, nonetheless, He is the same God! If he did it for my mom, He most certainly can do it for you, or the person you are thinking of right now.

To further show Himself faithful to her, on December 21, 2014, He would make a union that would take my mom's life to a height that was matchless and fostered a happiness and joy matched only by her love and devotion to Him! On that day she wed the "love of her life" (mom's words) in the person of James Kelsey Roberts, Jr. The ensuing three plus years were the best she experienced in her 62 years (her words again)! I had never seen my mother so happy and filled with joy. Dad James, I thank you for that! I am forever grateful for the way you loved our mother!

February 16, 2018

Mom was scheduled to have a procedure removing her defibrillator. I had always traveled to wherever she was when things like this would happen. But this time, mom was married and dad was there to stand where I always stood. I spoke to her before she went back, we prayed, and she made me remember all of the things she'd told me concerning her life insurance and wishes should something happen to her; as she'd done every time she had any type of procedure. Of course, I said OK. However, this time turned out to be much different. It would be unforgettably different in fact. The doctors encountered a complication during mom's procedure. They created a tear in her heart. More than an hour and a half would go by, then we had a family call with the surgeon and the assisting surgeon.

Mom's good friend Kim was there at the hospital with Dad, and she called me on the phone to be a part of the meeting with the doctors. What happened next changed my life forever. He told them, "We couldn't save her." It was as if I was having an immediate out-of-body experience. I could not breathe for a moment and I went numb. Simultaneously, I heard the saddest and most hurtful scream; one like I had not heard since my grandmother died. Grandma's funeral was the first time I saw or heard my grandpa Lucius cry. The scream I heard in that moment startled me. Then I asked Kim, "Who else is there with you and Dad? Who is that screaming?" She replied, "That's Dad!" My heart broke all the more. There was a pain in his cry, a hurt in his scream that's hard to describe.

I took a moment to cry, then my thoughts shifted to my brother Jay, and the short list of whom I needed to tell first. See, Jay was aware that mom was in surgery and they had run into some sort of complication, but he did not yet know mom had passed away. I told Kim and Dad I would handle telling Jay Jay, and for them not to take his calls or post anything on social media, so I could have time to get to Flint, MI. (an hour away) so he could hear this from me. I got to him just before he got beside himself due to them not answering his calls. When I told him mom had died, he lost it of course. Spewing angry explicatives, he started yelling at God. He actually said he hated God! I immediately interceded for him. He would soon calm down enough to listen to me and apologize for blowing up. He stated he didn't know what he was going to do. I said the same. But I encouraged him that we would make it through together.

The GMOAT

She will forever be the Greatest Mother Of All Time in my book! Of course, you only get one, but God knows I'm forever grateful that Denise Marie Fleming Jamerson Roberts was mine!

Mom was a Minister of Music my whole life. However, she also served as Evangelist and a Lead Pastor for several years. She was a proud member of Mt. Moriah Missionary Baptist Church, Savannah Georgia, where Dad still serves as the Senior Pastor. She was also a member of the Savannah Interdenominational Ministers Wives and Widows (SIMWW), and the founder of the Word Walking Women Ministry where the study of scripture and its application to daily life was paramount and something she enjoyed greatly.

My mother's redemptive story is amazing within itself. Maybe you know someone who has also had a similar life and need to be encouraged that deliverance is possible. God is an amazing father, and what He did for her, He will do for another mother or father that needs this type of deliverance and restoration.

> "[39]Return to thine own house, and shew how great things God hath done unto thee. And he went his way, and published throughout the whole city how great things Jesus had done unto him"
> **(Luke 8:39, KJV)**

I am so glad that I was able to repair the cracks and holes in our relationship many years before she left this earth. I thank God that I did not let the trauma of my childhood rule my heart and guide my life, and keep me from the beautiful relationship we enjoyed. She often told me I was the best of her. Those words still humble me. I am her legacy.

Her legacy will live forever! I am ensuring that! Stay tuned.

Chapter 2

Call Me Ishmael

[20] And as for Ishmael, I have heard thee: Behold, I have blessed him, and will make him fruitful, and will multiply him exceedingly; twelve princes shall he beget, and I will make him a great nation"
(Genesis 17:20, KJV)

My Beginning

Born to my mother and him while he was a married man, I can imagine how crazy things must have been for him. To have a wife and a lover pregnant at the same time must have been hard. To allow your wife to throw the baby shower for you and your lover's child must have been crazy. Certainly was brazen! To be on the verge of having two children born near the same time by two different women must have been wild!

In fact, my middle brother and I were born the same year nearly one month apart. He was born in September and me in October. Yet, all of this is not crazier than "My Biological" having started this affair with my mom when she was yet a minor. No, her initial age does not dissolve my mom of the part she played as she and I discussed so many times in both my teen years and adulthood, but it is the truth nonetheless.

From my first day out in the world, there was always that whispered question every time someone looked at me. Is Darty *******'s son? One of my favorite memories was of my mother explaining how my great-grandmother (My Biological's grandmother - MaDea) held me for the first time. See, my grandma Beatrice (my mom's mother) and my great-grandmother (Madea), were very good friends! I know right? Interesting, wouldn't you say? Anyway. When I was about 10 years old, my mother and grandparents explained that MaDea sent word to my mom through my grandmother to bring me over to see her when I was still an infant.

So, my grandparents and my mother loaded me in the car and drove me over to her house. She reached out and took me from my mother's arms and, after looking at me for just a moment, said "oh yeah, this is one of mine." I literally got chills as I wrote that last sentence. She knew after one look, that I was her blood and she never treated me otherwise for the rest of her days.

As I eventually grew, my features became all the more undeniable to people within the church and elsewhere. To the point that my mother was moved to tell me at an early age who my father was. Me not knowing the impact or weight of what she had just told me, I ran up the hall at our home church and said with a loud and exciting voice, "Hi Daddy!" Imagine the fallout from that for a moment, if you will.

Our home church would begin to gather in large numbers on a Sunday morning around 9:10/9:15am in preparation for Sunday School that began at 9:30am, and every generation attended in large numbers so there were a ton of people around. I can still remember my mother sitting me down when we got home to explain that I could not call him that. With tears running down her face, she would go on to tell me that he would not be my daddy like other daddies because he has a family already. That moment was when the emotional formation about my biological began. From that day, I began to learn to accept that I would always be the secret that many people knew of but never openly discussed. And the coming years would prove that to be true on many levels.

Along the Way

Over the years I would often ask myself why he did not want me. My mom would take it hard when she could not provide answers that would help me. However, she never spoke ill of him. Never. There were times in elementary and junior high school where I would act out. I can remember a time at Longfellow Middle School when I acted out on several occasions and told my grandpa Lucius I was angry that my dad did not want me. My grandfather consoled me as much as he could, but he'd always put his foot down. He'd say, "Boy, straighten up. You don't get to throw your life away because you feel like someone threw you away. You have the same chances to make something of yourself as anyone else does. So, whatcha going to do?" Yes, he said it just like that. I've never forgotten those words. I'll never forget how he would hold my hand, love me, guide me, and kick me in the butt at the same time! He was not going to let me get down on myself and make excuses to not give my best! Sure there have been times that I would still get down on myself and have a pity party, but his words would always ring in my head as motivation. They still do, even though he is no longer here with me.

He Called Me

There came a time that I wrote "My Biological" a letter. There had been an emotional event with my children and I felt no other recourse. After the letter was received and read, I get a call from my aunt (his youngest sister) and we discussed the letter and the whole story behind me, my birth, and whether I was his son or not. She then arranged for a conversation between he and I. So, he calls my cell while I was at work one day, and I cleared my calendar and found a vacant office to speak with him. Honestly, I was excited, nervous, happy, and angry all at the same time. Inside I was saying, "it took me sending a letter to you, your wife, your nephew, and your youngest sister, to get a call from you? Ironically, we never spoke directly about the reason I wrote the letter, but we did finally get to have a conversation about why he never sought to determine if I was in fact his son.

He had never acknowledged or owned me as his son. And I wanted to know why. I mean, if I potentially had a child out there that I didn't initially know was mine, I would move heaven and earth to make things right. So, I asked him why he had never taken action to answer the question once and for all. To this question, he gave the following reason for never having a paternity test: "Your mother told me you weren't my son." This was a true statement. My mother did tell him that. However, what he was not aware of was why she told him that at the time. According to my mother, "My Biological" is a terrible liar and his wife was always able to read him very well. So, in true Denise Marie fashion, my mother covered him and protected him by telling him I wasn't his son. That way he would be able to go to his wife and emphatically tell her what he believed to be the truth, and she would believe him. My mom would soon tell him the truth, but he didn't know she'd told me that fact when he offered his reasoning. When I told him that I knew she had later told him the complete truth, he was silent. Then he resolved to stick to the position that my mom told him I wasn't his and he offered nothing more. I thanked him for the call, he wished me well, and I wished him the same.

At the time I was aware that he and my mother had spoken months prior to our phone call. I did not tell him I knew of that conversation. My mother visited him at his church and the two of them spoke about me. Then when she strongly encouraged him to do right by me. By doing right by me, she meant that he should acknowledge me as his son.

Then, with tears running down his face, he gave the following reason why he couldn't: "Do you know what my Church will do to me if I tell them this now?" Personally, I think he was underestimating the forgiveness and Grace of the people in the church. Redemption is available, but you have to avail yourself to receive it. My mother always told me not to hesitate to go to him if he were to ever reach out and wants to see me. Of course, I agreed even though I struggled with that instruction. While I'm not holding my breath waiting on it to happen, because mom said it, I will honor it.

I Told You Girl

One Sunday I preached at Metropolitan Baptist Tabernacle in Flint, MI for their Youth Day. It was during the time shortly after Rev. Dr. A.J. Pointer had passed away and the church was in the process of a pastoral search. My mother was in town and came to play the organ for me. The service went well, and after the benediction I was down front of the pulpit receiving people and shaking hands as customary in a traditional Baptist Church. Then two ladies approached me together. Neither said a word for the first few seconds or so. They just looked at me, then looked at one another and smiled. Then, one of them just came straight out and asked me, "Is (they said "My Biological's" name) your father?" Without pause I said, "Yes ma'am."

One of them looked at the other and said, "I told you girl. He looks just like him." They would then share that they were members of his church and they had come to see me for themselves as they had heard of me for years. Let me be clear, although I've never sought to create discomfort for him or his family, I will never lie if asked if he is my father.

So, You're the Secret!

On May 24th Big Mama was laid to rest. May 24th happens to be my little brother Jay Jay's birthday. The funeral took place at "My Biological's" church. During the family hour and viewing, I could see people looking and wondering why so many people kept stopping to hug me and shake my hand during the funeral. I'm sure it was mainly because I was sitting near the rear of the church. To be exact, I was sitting 3rd row from the back.

During the eulogy, "My Biological" had the nerve to talk about single mothers being part of what's wrong with society. I believe he was attempting to paint grandma in a good light, as she was a phenomenal mother, but his words came off as a slap in my face to single mothers everywhere. My mother was a strong single mom and raised me well! Not to mention, she was a single mom, in part, due to his role. Then I could feel someone staring at me. Turns out it was my big brother's ex-wife. I looked over a few times and she was looking at me. So was their son. I'd later learn that I looked familiar to them. The funeral ends, and we're in the hall preparing to leave to go to the parking lot and "My Biological" comes out of his office and everyone sees it. He and I were dressed close to identically. We both were wearing cream suits, with cream French-cuffed shirts, and a soft pink necktie.

I encountered my brother's ex-wife in the parking lot while leaving. She came right up to me and said, "so you're the secret! I've heard of you for years and saw firsthand how angry your brother would get whenever you were brought up. It was a big secret. Now I see why." We exchanged numbers and she wanted my nephew to meet me and know who I was. We did not push an introduction as neither of us wanted to cause any issue within the family. I'd not been a part of his life up to that point, so there was no reason to force anything new. It would have only created conversations that no one really wanted to have.

Unwanted but Blessed

That experience following my grandmother's funeral was the closest I'd ever come to any form of relationship with "My Biological's" family, but causing uproar in his family was not the way I wanted to create connection. So I decided that I would not try to insert myself in any way. Don't mistake my words as me being those of great heart-felt consideration for him and his family, but rather words of wisdom accompanying a mindset that said I had made it this far in life without him so why try and force any form of relationship now. Not to mention, I felt that it would all probably be rejected and was honestly afraid to face that reality. So I just let all thoughts go.

I've found that the unwanted child is typically seen as a nuisance or an interruption. I never wanted that to be me. I have found myself going out of my way to not call out "My Biological" or cause him any shame. I don't say his name in this book for fear of retaliation or retribution, but in order to allow him to save face for his current reality.

I Chose Forgiveness

It was not until I was 39 years old that I finally came to terms with the suppressed bitterness that I had felt for so many years. In fact, it was a combination of bitterness, resentment, and hatred. Be careful of your rush to judge me. So many people are still stuck in the snare of bitterness, resentment, and hatred. Once I was aware that I had suppressed the feelings, I knew that therapy was the only way for me to deal with this once and for all. I knew I could not let the root of bitterness grow, now that I was aware of its existence.

Therapy was one of the best things that could have ever happened to me. I talked about my true feelings, found it in myself to forgive "My

Biological," and figured out why I had suppressed so much for so long. Then I came to the realization that nothing and no one is worth my peace of mind. Likewise, I will allow nothing and no one to cost me God's grace on my life. I came to terms a long time ago that "My Biological" did not want me, but moreover that his rejection of me, never altered my value to God. God saw me then and sees me now. He kept me then and keeps me now. He has guided me for as much as I would allow in manhood, fatherhood, being a mentor, and now as a spiritual leader. He always had a plan for me. Thank you, Lord for placing purpose in and around me from the start.

> "Make sure no one gets left out of God's generosity. Keep a sharp eye out for weeds of bitter discontent."
> **(Hebrews 12:15, Message)**

> "See to it that no one comes short of the grace of God; that no root of bitterness springing up causes trouble, and by it many become defiled;" **(Hebrews 12:15, NASB)**

Bitterness, resentment, and hatred never affect those for whom you harbor it. It never makes them lose weight, gain weight, fall into depression, or live in denial. However, it absolutely leads to some or all of those things in the life of the one who can't get beyond it all. Forgive and move on! It will be one of the most spiritually freeing experiences you ever have.

To "My Biological," I FORGIVE YOU! May these words free you from the secret demons you've lived with all these years. Blessings to you.

Chapter 3

The Son

"[18]Discipline your son while there is hope,
And do not desire his death."
(Proverbs 19:18)

Momma Didn't Play

My momma didn't play. I always knew it but I think my brain must have gotten stuck on "idiot" mode one day in 1982. I was in the 4th grade sitting in Mr. Evan's class. He was one of my all-time favorite teachers. This day, I'd finished my work activity and was supposed to be sitting quietly in my seat while my classmates were finishing theirs. Well, I didn't. I started horsing around with others who had also finished, but I went completely overboard. Back then, there were telephones in the classroom and I was doing my good class clowning that day. So, Mr. Evans called my mother, told her what I was doing, and left the phone off the hook so she could listen.

We lived 7 short blocks from our elementary school. We attended Martin Luther King, Jr. Elementary. Of course, my momma heard everything and when she'd heard enough, she walked to the school (from Jamieson St. to Rankin St.) picking a switch along the way. She showed up with rollers in her hair and a switch in her hand! She took me into the boy's bathroom (I'll never forget those baby blue ceramic tiled walls) and commenced to spank my behind real good. You could say she did her "good whipping" that day. I screamed to high heaven. The white teachers wanted to call the police, but the black teachers and the black principal told them to stand down. My momma said, "you embarrassed me, so I embarrassed you!" The old folks say, "where you show out, you get wore out." Needless to say, I was on the honor roll for the remainder of my elementary years!

Good Memories

I have so many fond memories of being a young boy. Probably one of the dearest memories I have is of family dinner for Thanksgiving. We would gather at my great uncle Albert and aunt Dora's house on E. Myrtle Ave. Uncle Albert was my grandfather's brother. In the same block as Metropolitan, the Church I was raised in. Grandma Beatrice would make her famous homemade rolls and she and aunt Dora would cook everything else together. Then we would move the couch in order to set up the long table. Oh the spread we would have! It would be aunt Dora, uncle Albert, grandma Beatrice, grandpa Lucius, Mrs. Odell Broadway (a close family friend), momma, Jay Jay, and me. We would eat, nap, then eat some more. Then we'd help clean up and make ready to head home. The rolls were always gone, but we always wanted more.

Then we would do it all again at Christmas, only it was hosted at grandma and grandpa Flemings home at 722 E. Lomita. Of course, there were the summer trips to Idlewild Michigan where we stayed in the cottage that grandpa Lucius, uncle Albert, and uncle Quincy had built by hand on Paradise Lake. I had no idea at the time (late 70's, early 80's) what it meant to be a black family owning lakefront property, let alone two motorboats and a rowboat. Idlewild, MI was a mecca for black people from the late 50's thru 80's. While many black people still own property there, a lot of development has taken place that moved land and property, once owned by blacks, to the ownership of non-blacks. It was always a family vibe when we were there. There were no strangers and everyone cared for and looked out for one another. Just thinking about those vacation experiences are nostalgic! That is a part of my childhood that I will cherish forever.

I'm Number 2

You've read of my beginnings in the previous chapters and dedication. However, what most people do not know is that my mother had a miscarriage of a baby girl, a few years prior to becoming pregnant with me. She was embarrassed to be pregnant, and she drank turpentine in order to lose the baby. She got so sick she thought she would die. She was so afraid and sorrowful that she promised God, if He allowed her to survive drinking the poison, that she would never abort another child.

When she learned she was pregnant with me, she remembered her promise and she kept it. My little brother did not even know this fact about mom. Remember mom told me almost everything. However, he knows now that he's read this book. We would have had a big sister. I would not have been the oldest. These are two thoughts I would often have not too long after mom told me this truth. It's cool being the oldest, but there were many times when I wished I were not and it's not always fun being the oldest, the strongest, the most responsible, the one everyone expects to have the answer, or the one everyone looks to for solutions to problems.

Mom would speak to me often of how she imagined our sister would be. She never gave her a name because she said it would have hurt more. But she would dream of her and then struggle to forgive herself. She said I always reminded her of the promise she made to God and that was an encouragement. You could say, I'm her fulfilled promise! It helped her stay grounded in some ways. Mom would finally forgive herself as she realized that God had indeed already forgiven her. I was so happy for her to get over that obstacle. I can only imagine how heavy that must have been for her. But in spite of and despite of all of the things that she faced, she came through it. Though some were self-inflicted, many were not.

You Never Would Have Known

A lot of evil things were spoken about my mom. To see and speak to her while she was out and about, or in front of hundreds of people, you would never have known because she did not carry it. But when she got home, I became more than her son, I became her confidant. I grew up pretty fast. Somehow mom knew I could handle it. Turns out she was right! Mom was usually right. She wasn't perfect but she was phenomenally my mom.

I was constantly amazed at how my mom did life though I did not always understand or like everything she chose to, or was forced to do. She never failed my brother and I. No matter the circumstance, we still won. It may not have felt like it at the time, it certainly was scary at times and we most certainly did not enjoy the process, but God never failed us. He never left us alone.

Our village was amazing. I knew more about who helped us at times than most kids my age would. Mom often brought me alongside of her in some adult situations. Unconventional? Yes. Did it work in our favor? Yes. Mom had more foresight than most, and absolutely knew what she was doing with me. Subsequently, I learned and knew more about life by the age of 13 than some adults knew at the time.

I remember us not having money for Halloween costumes one year. Mom had the amazing idea to grab old bed-sheets, cut them up, and make us into two of the three wise men that went to worship Jesus after His birth. My brother and I were so embarrassed to have to explain our costumes to everyone. What I know now, that I didn't know then, is that mom was a creative beyond my imagination, and that many people thought her shepherds costume idea was phenomenal. Of course, being in the 3rd and 5th grades, the last thing we thought was that it was a phenomenal idea. Then we wore them to our "Harvest Night" (Baptist Church folks know, we had this in place of a Halloween party at the church long before "Hallelujah" night became a thing) at the church that night and the costumes were a total hit! Those same costumes we were ashamed to wear to our elementary school, we were proud to wear to church and we boasted that mom had made them.

Nothing to Eat

For as much as mom loved and cared for Jay and I, we endured some hard times. I can remember the government cheese that you seemed to need volcanic heat to melt. I remember the powdered milk that almost always turned out as white water, but we fixed our minds to believe that it was close enough to real milk just so we could have a bowl of King Vitamin's cereal. I remember the peanut butter in the white can that had oil on top that you had to mix before you could eat it. For those that don't know firsthand, I just described the welfare commodities that people receiving food stamps or other state assistance would be given. I remember how embarrassed I would be when I had to go with mom to pick up those items. I remember seeing some of my elementary classmates from time to time, and being ashamed for them to see us. However, I never realized at the time that they were there for the same reason as we were.

I remember one time when the fridge contained nothing but a pitcher of water and the freezer a mystery something wrapped in foil. Likewise, the cupboards were pretty bare, with nothing but a few boxes of jiffy mix and a can of beets to be found. Jay and I were hungry and we told mom there was nothing to eat. She told us to go watch TV and she started clanking around in the kitchen. In about 25 minutes mom called us into the dining room to come eat. We had no clue what she could have found. After all, we saw nothing.

It turns out the mystery foil was some hamburger meat, that mom had frozen after using only part of it for another meal. So she thawed it, cooked it, and made a pan of cornbread. Then, after browning the meat, she added the can of beets to it. Then she spread the mixture of beets and hamburger atop of the pan of cornbread, sliced it in sections, and served it to us.

I saw her wiping tears from her eyes as she plated what she had made. Jay didn't notice her tears, but I did. She would later cry and apologize to me for us having to eat that, but it was all she had to give. I told her not to cry and that both of our stomachs were full.

I've never eaten beets since that day, but I will never forget that night. In fact, anytime I see a beet or someone mentions beets, I remember everything about that night. In all, what I remember the most is just how thankful we were to have a meal and that there was enough for both Jay and I to have our fill. I come from small and humble beginnings indeed.

> [10] For who hath despised the day of small things? for they shall rejoice, and shall see the plummet in the hand of Zerubbabel with those seven; they are the eyes of the Lord, which run to and fro through the whole earth. **(Zechariah 4:10, KJV)**

A Hard Lesson

During a time when my mom was in the deepest moments of her addiction, we were all living with grandpa Lucius. Grandma had passed on to Glory and things were really hard for mom. Actually, things were hard for all of us in some ways. One night Jay Jay was in the basement playing and watching TV and I was upstairs in the living room. This night we were all home and mom and granddad were having a hard conversation in the family room.

See, back in the day, kids were not allowed in the room when adults were talking. The dismissal from the space would often go something like this; "Y'all get out of here. Go play, grown folks are about to talk." Or if they started conversing not realizing kids were still in the room and then they saw you staring at them while talking they would say, "get out of my mouth and get out of here being grown!" Some of you reading this can totally relate to those statements.

Well, I heard my mom's voice rise. Then I heard granddad calmly say, "Denise, watch ya self." Then mom's voice rose louder and then I heard a loud "whack" sound and mom let out a short but loud scream. I ran into the family room to see that granddad had slapped my mom for being disrespectful. Mom then ran into the bathroom. I looked at the sofa where she was sitting and saw a wet spot on the sofa cushion. My granddad had literally "slapped the piss" out of my mom. So to everyone reading this, yes it can be done! A wave of emotions came over me as I realized what had happened. I was extremely upset because he'd hit my mom, but I was just as disappointed in her that she had disrespected him to that degree.

I had never heard my mother be disrespectful to my grandpa. She used to always say and show that she loved him so much! She would say he was her hero from the time she could remember. Her addiction had gotten the best of her and she lost herself in that moment. She expressed to me how ashamed she was for how she had behaved, they reconciled and they were close until his last day. It was during those days I saw her be the best daughter to him. It was during those years that I truly understood what it meant to be a son to her.

"**A Son**. This is something that I struggled with learning how to be. I used to think that a father had to do all the work, and that a relationship between a father and son fell mostly on the father because they are responsible for the son's existence. You have taught me that this is not the case at all. Being a true son is absolute WORK! You have to truly commit yourself be being a son. Show yourself that, whoever you call father, you can honor them in who they are and their own unique journey with Christ. You taught me that being a true son is not easy maybe one of the toughest things a man can do.

I truly honor and respect that way you continue to carry yourself when it comes to your relationship with your biological father knowing the effect that can have on a man and his children and it amazes me how you continue you rise. I've seen you submit yourself under other Men of God, already knowing the call that is on your life but never letting that distract you from the current assignment that was in front of you. Another lesson on remaining humble wherever you are." *William H. Murphy, IV, god son, Worship Leader, Walmart, Inc.- Team*

> "Lord, thou hast heard the desire of the humble: thou wilt prepare their heart, thou wilt cause thine ear to hear: To judge the fatherless and the oppressed, that the man of the earth may no more oppress."
> **(Psalm 10:17-18, KJV)**

With everything I experienced and endured while being raised by my mother, I still saw the best in her. I loved her more than I could have ever said with words. I trusted her second only to God. Mom, thank you for making me into the son I was.

Chapter 4

The Man

"[11] When I was a child, I used to speak like a child, think like a child, reason like a child; when I became a man, I did away with childish things"
(1 Corinthians 13:11, NASB)

To Prove Them Wrong

As an adult, although I'd learned right from wrong as a child, there was an element of my childhood that I had not dealt with. Remember in Chapter 2 where I quote my mother, "….My prayer is that God protect you and Jay from this life! I don't know what I would do if this lifestyle were to touch the two of you." This spoke to her fear that the homosexual lifestyle would somehow taint us. That was a real fear for mom then, and it's a real fear for many parents today. I want to also recall my mentioning what people would say about my mom sleeping in the bed with a woman and about her having a romantic relationship with a woman:

"So, from the 3rd grade until my freshman year of college, my mother chose to live a lesbian lifestyle."

This truth made me want to do all in my power for people to never think that I was, in any way, gay. So how does a young man try to prove his masculinity? Well, aside from fighting, or some other archaic form of expressing his testosterone, he seeks to conquer as many women as possible. So, the level of my promiscuity and how I went through women was at an all-time high in my late teens and early twenties. Many I remember, but many names I have long since forgotten. This behavior would last nearly 20 years! Sadly, I caused hurt to a number of women in many different ways during this span of my life. I cringe at the thought of a man hurting my daughters or goddaughters in such a way. I continue to caution them, as often as possible of the pitfalls of falling to fast for someone you don't truly know.

Soul-Ties

I discovered what soul-ties were and recognized how they were ruining my life because I had so many women walking around with pieces of me, and I with pieces of them. Spiritually we were connected and only a spiritual intervention would rectify this. I found myself acting out of character and saying things that were not even familiar to me. That, my friends, is exactly what soul-ties do to you. Think about it this way, the marriage vows speak to the two becoming one flesh. That's God's order. But when people go outside of His order and align or unify in a way God did not intend, they find themselves confused and spiritually scattered about.

I suffered from soul-ties to the point that I found myself battling a demon spirit called Succubus many nights, often experiencing sleep paralysis. I remember one morning, while getting my middle son ready for school, he says "dad you woke me up yelling and talking like you do at church." He meant I was speaking in tongues (my heavenly language) in my sleep. What he experienced was another battle with that demon spirit. I was intent on getting free, and breaking away from that way of living and thinking was a tough time for me. I had spiritually connected to so many women and I didn't know what I was in for when I let the enemy trick me into chasing what pleased my flesh. What I would come to learn is, not only was I spiritually connected to all of the women I'd laid with, but I was also spiritually connected to everyone they had laid with! Now that's a frightening realization, isn't it?

While I thought I was just using fornication and promiscuity to prove my masculinity, I discovered that I was also using it to mask my pain and vulnerability I felt from being abandoned by "my biological". I found that I was using it to over compensate for the self-perceived inadequacy and rejection I felt inside. In reality, I was unleashing a degree of darkness into and onto my life that would take me into an emotional and spiritual tailspin I could not have prepared for. I experience depression as I was trying to come out of that dark place. These battles were private and I was often alone in these moments.

God's plan has always been to enjoy sexual intimacy within the marriage union. It was never meant to be shacking, a common law, or a Live in situationship or entanglement. My deliverance helped me understand why so many relationships are a mess. Furthermore, it better taught me why parents always tell their children to be careful not to fall in love or get in relationships too young. See, the spiritual strength of a child (ages 13-18) is not prepared for the emotional and spiritual weight of relationships!

Heck, many older adults still aren't ready for that weight, if the truth were to be told. When young people fall in love they open a part of them that's not meant to be shared with everyone. All intimacy is not physical or sexual! Most times, it's emotional and spiritual first, and sometimes it never becomes physical.

I Came to My Senses

I found that losing my grandfather at an early age left a huge gap for a male role model in my life. Coupled with that was the fact that I hadn't forgiven "My Biological" yet but didn't know it then. However, I'd taken the position that any man not "My Biological" could only love me to a point and I could only trust them to a point! My reasoning was simple; how could I believe anyone loved me and wanted the best for me when the man who was bound to me by DNA refused to even acknowledge I was his son? I know now that was unfair, but with maturity comes wisdom and I'm older and wiser now. I hurt so many people that genuinely cared for me because I could only see their love through the lenses I viewed "My Biological" through.

Then these words rang out in my head: "At the end of the day son, you only have your word and your name. If your word is worthless, so goes your name." That's what my grandfather Lucius taught me from an early age. What I did not know then was that he was helping me learn who I was, and who I could be. I remain grateful for what he instilled in me. Although I struggled with rejection from "My Biological," grandpa Lucius never failed to tell me I was valued and loved. Ultimately, I became the man I am today because I never forgot everything he instilled in me. Although I had a forgetful spirit at times, I always regained my senses. Sadly, from my grandfather's generation to my children's generation, many fathers and grandfathers have not affirmed a great deal of boys and girls.

Subsequently, those boys and girls became men and women who had no real clue as to who they were. Thus, their identity was never fully established. From a Biblical perspective, Jacob (Israel) should be our example:

> "[14] And Israel stretched out his right hand, and laid it upon Ephraim's head, who was the younger, and his left hand upon Manasseh's head, guiding his hands wittingly; for Manasseh was the firstborn.
>
> [20] And he blessed them that day, saying, In thee shall Israel bless, saying, God make thee as Ephraim and as Manasseh: and he set Ephraim before Manasseh.
> [21] And Israel said unto Joseph, Behold, I die: but God shall be with you, and bring you again unto the land of your fathers."
> **(Genesis 48:14, 20, 21, KJV)**

Jacob (Israel) refused to die before he could lay hands on his sons and his grandsons. He wanted to bless them, tell them who they were, and who they were destined to be. He wanted to speak life and pass blessings down to the coming generations. I've tried

> "Where can I start? **A real man**. Someone I can truly admire and look up to. Someone in more ways than one I can aspire to be like. Just to name a few things that you are: **A Man of God**! Someone that I can say is truly after Gods own heart. He's someone that doesn't just wear the cross around his neck, but one who carries it on his back. A believing and a praying man! You're a preacher, but you don't allow that to over shadow who your are as a person. I've seen you believe and walk in faith even when others may have not understood your walk, but you believe in your own unique journey that the Lord has prepared for you."
> *William H. Murphy, IV, god son, Worship Leader,*
> *Walmart, Inc. – Team*

As a man, yes, I've made mistakes, yes, I've had some amazing victories and yes, I've had huge let downs. However, in all of these experiences, I have learned to guard my spirit. I am a man created in God's image and likeness, and that alone is why the enemy seeks to challenge my faith! But I boldly proclaim who I am! I declare that I am the head and not the tail. I am on top and not beneath! I am God's man, and I am the victor because of my faith in Jesus. This is the same declaration I have made and continue to make over my children. The enemy cannot have my life, he cannot have my children, and he cannot steal the purpose from my bloodline or my generations to come.

"¹⁰A thief is only there to steal and kill and destroy. I came so they can have real and eternal life, more and better life than they ever dreamed of" **(John 10:10, MSG)**

Chapter 5

The Father

"As a father has compassion on his children, so the Lord has
compassion on those who fear him."
(Psalm 103:13)

Man, I'm a Dad

I biologically became a dad at the age of 19. It was August 27, 1993, to be exact. Almost two months exactly prior to my 20th birthday. There were so many things surrounding this life-changing event. 1. I'd been unfaithful to my girlfriend of 3 ½ years at the time. 2. The woman I was seeing became pregnant. 3. There was the question of another guy who was in the picture and I was unclear as to how long he'd been in the picture.

Needless to say, I was all over the place and not necessarily in the best frame of mind walking into fatherhood. However, the thoughts that ruled my mind and provoked my actions were less about the validity of the twins conception, but more about the fear that had gripped me for the prior nine months! The fear of becoming a father after not having been truly fathered myself. Often, I asked myself, how can I expect to be a father, as I was not fathered? Sure, my grandfather was an amazing factor in my life. Heck, he was my father for 14 years! My mentors instilled great attributes in me, but there remained a fear and void that was yet to be revealed in me. Without that revelation at the time, I was floundering in this new space called fatherhood.

Parents know, but people who do not have children do not understand the pressure. They can speculate, but that's all it is, speculation. There is no "how to" manual, there is no "best practices" guide to how one operates as a good parent, or what being a good parent means. Nonetheless, you are expected to know the best things to do and to offer, no excuses. Well, I failed at all of those in the beginning. I loved but I was a horrible communicator. I was selfish. I wanted my life to basically stay the same, although I'd never have admitted that then. Honestly, I didn't even know that's how I was feeling at the time. Then, just a little over a year later, I had another son by my longtime girlfriend. Yes, she took me back even after I'd cheated and had the twins as a result. We'd broken up several weeks prior to learning that she was even pregnant. However, the knowledge of her pregnancy would not have prevented the breakup. We'd already grown apart. But unlike the first pregnancy that made me a father, this time I was there as much as possible. With work, and not having a car, I did all I could to be present and not make the same early mistakes I'd made with my twins. However, my efforts to be better were seen by many as showing favoritism to her and my new son. There were so many exaggerations, embellishments, and flat out lies spoken regarding the amount of support I was providing.

Setting The Record Straight

In comes my mom. Unbeknown to me, she called a meeting with the two mothers, sat them down, and did her best to bring some clarity to what I was and was not doing as a father. In that sit down, she expressed that I shopped at Goodwill and Salvation Army. My new son's mom explained that I was indeed "not" giving her all of my money. She shared that I was giving what I could financially, but, moreover, I was giving as much of my time as I could, as that is what I had the most to give. What no one knew was that I would walk nearly 4 miles to my job at McDonalds on South Dort Hwy. No one knew that the State of Michigan was deducting 55% out of every one of my paychecks before I ever saw it. Imagine working 80+ hours at $11 per hour, and more than half of it be gone before you ever see your check. Yet, I was still expected to maintain a place to stay, a mode of transportation, and feed myself, while still doing other things the kids needed.

No one knew that it was all I could do to pay rent and my cricket phone bill. No one knew that I was shopping at the Goodwill for my clothes because it was all I could afford. There was no extra! It never mattered that people didn't know where my clothes came from, but it was always humorous to me the stories people would come up with.

I've been my own barber since I was 14 years old, so I didn't have that expense. I took pride in my appearance, so I was always clean and well groomed. There were even people who did nice things for me just because they wanted to be a blessing. However, people who had no clue often determined that they were purchases I'd managed to make for myself. This sit down led by my mother was an attempt to set the record straight and to make things a bit smoother for me. I'm not sure if it actually helped since I did not learn about the sit down until many years later.

That's the way my mom would move. She would help you at times and you wouldn't even know it. Seeing you in a better condition meant more to her than you knowing she helped you get there. That's just who she was.

The Real MVP

Several years would pass. Things would level off a bit and my responsibility would rise to a respectable place. My middle son's grandmother would pass away and his mom would ultimately decide to move to Georgia. However, she would make a decision that would impact both his and my life forever. She allowed our son to choose whom he would live with. Mind you, he is only in the 3rd grade at the time. Before we let him choose, she sat me down to talk. She told me, "I know how you came up and I would never just take him away from you because I know what being a father means to you."

I was in tears, of course, and completely blown away at such a gesture. Then came the talk with him, and ultimately the choice was given. When asked if he wanted to go with his mom and move to Georgia or stay here with me, my son chose me. It broke her heart! What mother would not be heart-broken? Yet, her next move made her the real MVP in my book. She honored his choice and let him stay. That will forever be one of the most unforgettable moments of my life. The joy I felt in my heart was indescribable. She had done something that I could only repay by bringing him up and preparing him to be a respectable young man. She didn't take my son from me. But moreover, she trusted me to father him. That, in and of itself, was all the motivation I needed to live up to my own hopes for myself as a father.

She would move to Georgia and I would become a single father in every aspect of the term. She was very much in touch and even arranged for a direct deposit to hit my account each of her pay periods. I always told him where the extra money came from and made sure he went to visit her as much as possible. I always found it funny how so many people would be taken back by her choice to let him stay and her financial support, as if it was wrong. I struggled with this for a period, but then the reality set in that single moms and single dads are not equal in the eyes of public opinion. I must admit that is a double standard I didn't see coming, considering the circumstances of my being a single father were identical to most, if not all, single moms I knew growing up.

He Ran Away

After a few years, my middle son would decide that he wanted to go to Atlanta to live with his mother. He missed her, it had been a few years since she'd moved and I was a tough father. I only knew one way. My mom was tough on my brother and I. Nonetheless; I encouraged him to go and was supportive. He would move to Atlanta and immediately he struggled in school. He couldn't stay focused and his grades were suffering. It so happened that his school did not have organized sports and neither his mother nor her boyfriend had the time or capacity (because of work) to take him to league sports activities. The congested traffic makes commuting take "forever" to get from one side of Atlanta or suburbs to another, so it is extremely difficult to keep kids in sports programs, as they could be a great distance away.

In contrast, he thrived in school while with me, but I believe it was because he loved sports and that was his outlet. Not to mention I had a rule in my home that I'd learned from one of the best coaches I'd watched growing up. He would say, "no books, no looks." Meaning, if my grades weren't up to par, I couldn't play sports. If their grades were acceptable, I made it a point to keep my boys engaged and equipped to participate in every sport they were excited about. Well, in the absence of sports as an outlet, he would continue to struggle. He wasn't happy and no one there seemed to be able to reach him.

One day I get a call from his mother while I was at work and what she said to me arrested every emotion I had inside. She said, Darty, Mishad (his middle name used as his nickname) is missing. I froze! I was immediately numb! He had been gone almost a whole day and his friends did not know where he was. They said they had not seen him. I walked directly into my then boss' office at the Greater Flint Health Coalition, and told him I had to leave. I told him I was getting a one-way ticket and was not coming back until I found him. At the time I did not possess a credit card and did not have enough money to buy the plane ticket to Atlanta. In comes my god-mother (Brenda Floyd) to purchase the ticket and tell me that whatever she could do to help me, she would. I would fly to Atlanta that day with the intention of staying until I found my son.

I arrived to the subdivision where he and his mother lived, and still no word from or sign of him. I was anxious, angry, nervous, worried, afraid, and full of adrenaline all at once, but all we could do was pray and wait.
I went outside when I saw kids tossing a football around. I called them over and asked if they knew my son. They were hesitant because I was a stranger, but one of them was looking at me hard and asked, "Are you his dad?" I said yes, I am. He said, "You look like him." I said, if any of you know where he is, tell him his father is here! Tell him I came to find him. I then told them to give me some dap so they could tell him they saw and touched me.

What I didn't know at the time was that one of those kids was hiding my son in their basement. So, the kid who was hiding him runs back and tells my son I was there. At first, he didn't believe him, but then the boy told him, "I touched him". Though my son was skeptical, after a little while he would come home. I read him the riot act, yelled, asked him what the hell was he thinking, hugged and kissed him, and cried all at the same time. I've never been filled with a wave of fear, relief, and joy all at once. My son would later tell me, Dad I knew you would come get me." So, I cried some more! I later learned that the young man's grandmother loved my son and didn't think anything was strange that he had been there all day as he was there so often with their family. I would not wish the feelings I experienced on anyone. Not even an adversary.

I Did It Grandaddy

After my middle son had lived with me for a period of time, my twin son would begin to ask to come stay with his brother and me. It did not happen right away. My relationship with his mother was not as amiable as the one I had with his younger brother's mother. However, his pleas would wear on his mom and she decided to allow him to come. Then not too long after that, she would allow his twin sister to come live with us as well. Now I'm a single father with all three of my children living with me. I was more than thankful that God had been exceedingly faithful to me.

Yes, I had all 3 of my children under one roof but I was just as grateful that God had blessed me with the roof. I'd recently purchased my first home; a three-bedroom Cape Cod, with hardwood floors throughout, as well as a brand-new Grand Am right off the lot. No co-signer for either and I had no job at the time. Yes, you read that correctly. When the process started, I was working but then was laid off shortly after. I'll never forget the personal banker I had. She was a Christian woman who watched me some nights having my boys with me doing their homework, while I was attending my home ownership classes.

I remember when she called me and said they were ready to close on the house. It was weird because I'd told her I'd lost my job. She said, well you have 60 days before your first mortgage payment. I was stunned! I put on a suit, drove to her office, and cried the entire signing. I got the keys, and drove straight over to the house. I was alone and I walked through the house and prayed. I went downstairs and there was only an empty painter's bucket. I flipped it over, sat down, and just cried. I imagined how proud my grandfather Lucius would be of me. I screamed out "I did it granddad, I did it"!

I was winning as they say. Yet, with this happening to and for me, I could not help but feel that there was still a void. However, I pushed through like my grandfather always told me to do. I was maturing, and with maturity comes, wisdom they say. I would still make mistakes as a son, a man, a father, and even as a mentor but I never stopped moving forward.

The Hurt

One day, something happened that would not allow me to suppress my bitterness and unforgiveness for "My Biological" any longer. My three babies and I went to the Genesee Valley Mall to do a little shopping. Wasn't a shopping spree by any means, but we grabbed a few things. Each one of them had a bag of their own. Then, as we're leaving the mall, they all get in the car. My daughter called front seat and the boys climbed in the back seat. Everyone gets strapped in and my daughter got to choose where we'd eat dinner. She chose Ruby Tuesdays. I'll never forget. As we're pulling out of the parking lot, her twin brother asks me, "so dad, your daddy never bought you a happy meal?" It seemed so random at the time, but I guess his little mind was connecting the dots from the answers I'd given to the questions they would ask sometimes.

I turned to look at him in the back seat and I said, "the way you feel right now son, I've never known how that feels." About 10 seconds later, I hear him sniffling and crying. He was crying for me! We'd just left the mall and were heading to a restaurant to have dinner. I've never known that feeling with my "My Biological". That hurt my son's feelings and he cried for me. I was instantly angry! Angry that "My Biological" had the power to hurt my children through his rejection of me.

The Letter

I was irate! It was unacceptable that "My Biological" had the power to hurt my son! To hurt all of them in fact, because they were all crying when it was all said and done. At that moment I made up in my mind to tell him how I felt. After dinner I called my mom and shared with her what had happened. I told her how angry I was and that I'd decided to write "My Biological" a letter. She told me to wait until I had calmed down. I did. I would sit down that night and write him a letter. The letter (a little over a page in length), shared the exchange with my son, expressed my anger and hurt by his refusal to acknowledge me as his son and how his absence from my life had led to so much hurt and sadness. I asked him why he'd never reached out or taken steps to settle any question about me being his son. I also was very clear that my letter was not to ask for a single thing aside from answers. Then, to ensure that he received the letter, or was at least aware of it, I sent a copy to him at his church and his home.

I addressed the letter sent to the church, to him; while I addressed the letter sent to his home to his wife. I also sent a copy of the letter to his oldest nephew and to his youngest sister. My reasoning for going to this extent was so that there was no confusion about the intent of the letter. After all, I'd been this huge secret and I was not willing to open myself up to being painted in a way that made me look like I had a hand out. I just wanted answers. As I shared in chapter 2, he would call me in response to my letter.

For the record, I have never asked him for anything in my life. Not one thing. However, just after my twins were born, unbeknownst to me, my mom went to him and asked him to help me get a job with General Motors (GM). If you don't know, GM has (or had) a referral program that pretty much gets you to the front of the line for hiring. Back then, he had such pull that he could have submitted a referral and I would have never known it was from him. He told her no.

My mother did not tell me she had asked him for this for me until the twins were maybe 10 years old. Yet, she still never spoke ill of him to me. Again, that's who she was.

Father And Protector

I was never my children's friend. I always pursued a strong meaningful relationship with them, but drew the line at becoming friends! That holds true still to this day. Here's why I say this. When you put yourself or allow your children to put you in the friend zone, there is the absence of well-established boundaries and true discipline, and disrespect will soon follow.

Just think about the things you did when you were young or not so young with your friends. How many of those things did you not want your parent (most likely your mom) to know about? My kids didn't really care for this philosophy when they were young. I found that it was more because of how their friends were being raised. My home was different and I was unapologetic about it. I didn't look down on their friends, but I did not want my children to become statistics. So, I was harder than many other parents. God intended for me to father and protect them, and early on I knew I would have to say no some of the times when they wanted me to say yes. I hated when they would be upset with me, but I could live with it if it meant I was keeping them safe.

On two occasions my two older sons wanted to go out and I said no. The first occasion was to just hang out with friends in the neighborhood, and they were upset that I said no. The next morning, the main friend they planned to hang out with was found shot to death in the street just two streets over and two blocks up from our home. The second occasion was to attend a house party. My oldest son pleaded to go. I could see the disappointment and anger in his face when I said no. The next morning, one of the most popular varsity football players that he played with was found shot to death in his car. Everyone loved this kid! His dad was an amazing father and football coach! I respected him greatly and so did many others. Both times, Holy Spirit said not to let them go. So, I listened. I recognized what my sons did not. That being, a few moments of satisfaction from going out on those two instances, could have led to a lifetime of regret for themselves, for me, and for their moms.

For as much as I love them, there have been some hard and some regretful exchanges between all of my children and me over the years. Some have been more hurtful than others. Some may have been preventable and some weren't. Nonetheless, I have always owned my errors. Not everything was for them to know and understand at young ages. I expressed as much. I was resolved to let my children be children. I've offered to all of them to have whatever conversations as adults that they may desire, but I've been very clear that there are elements or facts that they should prepare themselves to hear that they have never heard. To date, I have not been asked to have any of those conversations and I'm fine with that. My door remains open. We converse regularly enough about life, careers, and family, and I'm thankful for where our relationships stand. They are the arrows in my quiver and I am a blessed man to be their father.

> "[3]Lo, children are an heritage of the Lord: and the fruit of the womb is his reward. [4] As arrows are in the hand of a mighty man; so are children of the youth. [5] Happy is the man that hath his quiver full of them: they shall not be ashamed, but they shall speak with the enemies in the gate"
> **(Psalm 127:3-5, KJV)**

The God Children

My godchildren's list has always grown on its own. I actually only have five (5) godchildren whose parents actually asked me to be their godfather. The other seven (7) appointed me on their own and their parents accepted it and began to acknowledge me as such in their lives. Many of them have loving fathers who were not only present in their lives, but present in the home. This fact always bewildered me at first. It was somewhat of a regular occurrence that I would draw young people from both sides of the line if you will. Some who were from broken or single parent homes and some who were from two-parent homes. I can remember having very confrontational conversations with two fathers in particular after they heard their children refer to me as dad the first time.

Today, I continue to have healthy relationships with both of these fathers
We often laugh about that first discussion we had. Many years ago, I begin
calling this unique relational yet spiritual gift, a "Father's Anointing." No
to try and create a special tag for myself, but because so many young
people would just start to call me dad after various periods of time of me
pouring into them spiritually and emotionally. Each of these unique
relationships began because I was always able to listen AND hear them
Contrary to many beliefs, these are not the same action.

Let me be clear, I never discussed or requested that any of those tha
appointed me as their godfather call me dad. Not a single one. They all did
it on their own. Each time it took me off guard and raised my level o
humility based on how sacred that title is in my own life. That's not a term
of endearment I hand out easily, neither is the term friend, so I carry those
titles with care.

"**A FATHER!** This is the most influential part for me. The love
that you have for all of your children, that being biological and
spiritual, is something to always pay attention to. The spirit o
fatherhood that you walk in is unmatched! Your love is clearly
given and shown, in both easy and difficult situations. The love and
correction that comes with the way that you father, the lessons tha
are learned I will always appreciate. I honor the father you are and
the fatherhood that is on your life. I can only hope to be the kind o
father that you are and that my children will be able to feel the
fatherly love that all of your children do.

A Husband! I have got to witness firsthand the type of husband
you are. I can remember on your wedding day, in your vows, the
way you spoke about how your wife completed you. I admire the
way you continue you honor your wife, when things are great and
even when they may not be so great. You taught me how importan
communication is with your spouse, and how it is imperative tha
both parties as they grow together, continue to heal together as wel

as the danger when one heals and the other does not. I've always taken notes from you when it came to marriage because I know that I aspire to be married one day. It may be small to others but I love when you take the pulpit, you never fail to mention and honor the woman who stands beside you. It's my prayer that you continue to have a marriage that will thrive!

Lastly, how I see you as a **Friend**. You've always told me that you don't have many friends, and that you weren't meant to. You've always told me that you could count your friends on your hands. As someone who doesn't claim to have many friends either, I've learned from you the value of true friendship and what it means.

I'll always keep in mind the conversations we've had where you told me certain people where not my friends; that sometimes I have to love people from a distance, and how some are only out to receive what you can give them and never intend to add to you. Today I find peace and am content with having a handful of friends.

The thing that I may admire most about you, is how you will always admit to your mistakes. That may sound cliché, especially among those who take the pulpit to preach. They often fail to preach on their imperfection and it gets old because these same people never own their stuff. I've seen you admit to making a mistake and bounce right back, walk in your imperfections and mistakes and be able to heal!

To be healed and to be whole are my main goals in life and you taught me how to reach for healing.

You are truly a blessing from God and because I have you that's proof God loves me and He never intended for me to be alone. You are an answered prayer. You are a check in every box. Man, with all that being said I love you! And I can only hope to become a man

of God, father, husband, son and friend that makes you proud!
Sincerely,
Your son, William"

William H. Murphy, IV, god son,
Worship Leader, Walmart, Inc. – Team

"⁶ Train up a child in the way he should go: and when he is old,
he will not depart from it." **(Proverbs 22:6, KJV)**

"Fathers, do not provoke your children to anger, but bring
them up in the discipline and instruction of the Lord."
(Ephesians 6:4, KJV)

The boy who was a son, became a man, then a father, then a mentor, then a preacher, and then a husband, had many lessons over the span of my life. I'm glad that I learned from those lessons. Sure, I failed at times along the way, but overall, I learned what to do, what not to do, and how to teach my children and others how to sidestep some of those same pitfalls. I'm still learning today.

Chapter 6

The Mentor

"One good mentor can be more informative than a college education and more valuable than a decade's income."
-*Sean Stephenson*

This Work is a Calling

Having started in youth ministry as the leader of the Boys 2 Men Ministry at the New Jerusalem Full Gospel Baptist Church in Flint, MI., I have seen a great deal of young men over the years. Deacon Henderson Allen, Elder Marqus Harris, DeAndre Chilton, Sr., and myself, did our best to bring the boys (ranging from the age of 5 to 18) up with the principles of Respect, Discipline, and Responsibility being the standard. We taught them that these principles were standards to be applied to all things dealing with life.

I had five true mentors growing up. My grandfather, Lucius, Mr. John Rhymes, James Jarrett, Pastor John Thornton, and my oldest and favorite cousin, Charles Montgomery. I attempted to pattern my life after all of the things they instilled in me. Every young person I have ever had the privilege to serve and lead, got the best I could give at all times. Being entrusted as a mentor is not a light thing. This is a position of power to influence. To help guide an individual's life to the degree of which they desire to allow you, must be taken seriously and handled with care. There were other mentors that made significant deposits over the years, and almost daily I reflect on the contributions they have had in me becoming the man I am today.

Me being able to connect with my own mentees as well as my godchildren, on multiple levels, due to my own life's experiences have made it natural to operate in and be successful in this space. Likewise, this level of connection should be the goal of every mentor. Over time, I have grown to understand and appreciate the anointing that God placed on my life. The fact is, it was not just to do youth and young adult ministry, but intergenerational/multi-generational ministry. Yes, it is something I enjoy, but, moreover, it is my calling.

Motivate and Encourage

Being a mentor is a role that many have relegated to famous people, athletes, and others of the sort. However, at an early age, I found that I was unknowingly motivating and encouraging many from my position as a Youth & Young Adult Pastor. Of course, there are some that requested my mentorship, while other relationships developed out of the nature of my Levitical office. While I have put into words the impact that mentorship, motivation, and/or encouragement has had on my life, it's only my perspective. Allow the following quotes relative to my mentorship, motivation, and/or encouragement to provide a myriad of perspectives. These quotes are from those who watched me grow through struggle, those whom I have served or served alongside of, or worked with professionally:

"I was introduced to Dartanyan over twenty (20) years ago by, at the time, my significant other who is now my wife. I knew from the start that we would become close friends. I honestly believe it was God's plan to place us together. I was working with maximum secure juveniles and Darty literally had a strong passion for the youth of the church. I will never forget the first meeting for our mentoring program, Boys 2 Men Ministry. For the first meeting we were not anticipating a large turn out, but God had a trick for us. There were over thirty (30) young men from six (6) to eighteen (18) years of age in this small Sunday school classroom. The group included his own two (2) sons. Darty and I step outside for a quick second and looked at each other while laughing saying, "what are we going to do with all these boys."

That was a start of something special. Through his leadership, he helped mold those young boys into men literally. The way he carried himself around those young men made it was okay for a young man to be Saved, that it was okay to know the word of God at a young age and still rock Timberland boots, jerseys, and gold chains. Dartanyan taught those young men that they had the power to change the narrative about young black males coming from single-family homes in the city of Flint. Because of his passion and dedication to those young men, many have become college graduates, some have become husbands and fathers, and even business owners."

Henderson "Hendu" Allen,
Friend, Masters Graduate of The University of Michigan, Deacon
at New Jerusalem Full Gospel Baptist Church, Mentor

"When looking for a mentor you look for them to be well balanced and that's what my god dad is. He's judgment free, always giving the honest truth, as well as giving the Biblical aspect and the tools needed to help you move forward. He will tell you the hard truths and explain how to except them/deal with them, while also giving discipline and holding you accountable. He has talked me off the ledge and calmed my emotions plenty of times. There is nothing and I mean NOTHING I cannot go to him about, good, bad or embarrassing. If I text or call, no matter what time it is or what he's facing in his personal life, he's always present!

God couldn't have given me a better mentor to help me navigate life! Even with the amazing parents I have, it's still nice to have an outside person to go because sometimes talking with your parents can be difficult. He's even encouraged me to be more open with my parents in certain areas where I was afraid before. With the young girls that cling to me for advice and just need a listening ear he is the standard I hold myself for the kind of mentor I need to be. He's the best mentor there is. If you don't have one, get one because mine has impacted my life more than I could ever thank him for! He's a man of God, man of integrity, he isn't perfect and he will make that known, but he does his best by everyone he knows!"

Kiana Brown,
god daughter, Bachelors Graduate of the University of Michigan,
International Youth Ministry Admin, Step/Dance Team Leader

"Love. Selfless. Relational. Leader. Service. Wisdom. Heart. Integrity. All words I use to describe Dartanyan, the man, the father, the son, the pastor, the mentor, and the friend. He is the perfect blend of all the above to quench the thirst of a child in need of a father, to overfill with pride the heart of his loved ones, to be one of God's most trusted shepherds, to turn strangers into longtime compadres, and to inspire, guide, and challenge others to be better. He has certainly inspired, guided and challenged me to be a better version of myself over the years. I'm better spiritually, personally, and professionally.

Now, Dartanyan doesn't call many a friend, so I count it an honor to have that title. Being his friend challenges me to constantly self-reflect, self-improve, and grow. My friend has been my pastor when I've needed spiritual counsel and support. He has been the ideal leader I aspire to become. He has shown me how to nurture and feed into my relationships. He has shown me the difference between service that is selfless, verses service that is selfish. He has taught me that being vulnerable and humble is where true power resides. The list goes on, but the bottom line is I have witnessed him be the model person, leader, and friend I learn from even when he isn't trying to teach."

Wanda C. Brown,
Friend, MBA Graduate of Baker College, Bursar – Mott
Community College, Owner of Born To Sparkkle, LLC

"When it comes to mentoring youth, and adults for that matter, Dartanyan is definitely in the element he was created for. He has a heart for leading and guiding people. He has an innate ability to reach beyond the rough layers of the most difficult people and get them to produce the gifts and talents they were born with. Working side by side with him with our church youth program was an experience that I will never forget. Dartanyan's leadership even helped shape my own ability to lead. His impact on the lives of the individuals he mentors can be seen the moment he crosses paths with a former mentee. Dartanyan was built for this!"

DeAndre Chilton, Sr.
Friend, Bachelors Graduate of the University of Michigan,
Member of Alpha Phi Alpha Fraternity, Inc., Mentor for Alpha
Esquires of Flint, MI

"Mentor by definition is an experienced and trusted adviser. More often than not they're someone whose life has given them insight into certain roles and experiences that one may seek to understand. Navigating life isn't as easy as it seems but when you have someone willing to go out of their way to stretch you and usher you to an elevated way of approaching life you've found one of God's greatest assets on earth. They are what all of us should be for each other.

From Phil Jackson to Michael Jordan or Kobe Bryant, the greatest mentor is someone who sees the game from the outside, can recognize a double team being set up and can put a big enough bug in your ear to have you execute as if you thought of it on your own. The power of compelling ones to access their own glory is evident in the role of a great mentor.

The beckoning of a son rejected by his father, to a son alongside his brother willing to fight their father that accepted and cherished them, showed me more than I could ever know about what a great mentor looks like and how he acts. You were and are that mentor. Gifting someone with the experience of having a second Father when you've longed for your own Father is widely overlooked. How can a mentor like that ever be replaced?

Seeing you dad, the same rejected son, embrace his children and children that aren't yours shows men like myself that God has always and will always be the center of all things. When looking at the etymology of "mentor," the name perhaps ultimately means "adviser," because in form it is an agent noun of mentos "intent, purpose, spirit, passion". I grew up being raised by Abraham."

Alvin Claybrooks II,
god son, Graduate of Specs Howard of Media & Arts, Musician,
DJ, All-around Creative

"I have known Dartanyan Tymar Jamerson whom I call "Darty" and refer to as my brother for over 40 years and to truly know him is to love him. As kids Darty has always been a leader among many and he has never been afraid to tell his stories of survival, and I believe that avenue caused many youth and young adults to gravitate to him, and it has also allowed Darty to not only mentor young minds but to also minister to them.

This book is a testimony to all that no matter the circumstances, with God all things are possible. God has instilled a gift in Darty to reach people across all generations. Darty has not lived the "perfect" life and he has acknowledged that in the book, but he has strived to honor God and his family, and God has rewarded him in his endeavors. This title says it all. Call me Ishmael…

    -God will hear (Hebrew)
    -father of 12 rulers
    -lead a great nation"

Nikki Floyd McZee, god sister, Masters Graduate from Northern
Arizona University and University of Phoenix President – Bishop
Odis A Floyd Memorial Foundation, Owner - Floyd McZee
Financial Consulting

"Mentoring, Modeling, and Motivating are foundational pillars in which Dartanyan T. Jamerson stands on and operates in during his everyday life. Dartanyan has impacted a population of multi-generational people where his simple presence and influence can have the potential to catapult them to greatness and success in life. This father, friend, husband, and pastor expertly navigates through life with integrity, love, and honor. Darty has made it his life's work to support and encourage people to manage their own learning curves to achieve maximum happiness in all human endeavors and live up to their full potential. DJ is a friend that will be there in the good times, bad times and the just because times!"

Elder Marqus A. Harris,
Friend, Masters Graduate from Michigan State University,
Member of Kappa Alpha Psi Fraternity, Inc., Mentor

"For 16 years you've walked out this thing called life with me. From my relationships, to my faith, to my emotions; through life itself, you've provided us with so much wisdom. To me, one of the greatest lessons that you've taught us is that **"we may be the only Jesus that some people may ever see" (Pastor DJ).** You've walked this out in many different ways. I've seen you go above and beyond to connect with people. For example, I'll never forget when we went to see your tenants and you were communicating with them in sign language, which you learned from their children.

I've seen you pay for breakfast for a family out of the kindness of your heart and you being attentive to the Holy Spirit even though they may not have needed it. You're also one of the greatest leaders that I know. John Maxwell describes a leader as "one who knows the way, goes the way, and shows the way."

56

You've definitely done your part in showing us the way and I know I can speak for all of us when I say that we are the people we are today because your pour and your yes."

Jaice Harvey,
god daughter, Attended Central Michigan University,
International Youth Ministry Admin Assistant

"When most people think of a mentor, they think of the hands-on leadership and direction of someone who helps as a guide. You've been that over and over again. You've made sure that I intentionally put money in my savings.

You've allowed us on international platforms we never would've thought to ask to have. We've had leadership positions at young ages where adults actually listened to what we had to say because of your recommendations. All of this is appreciated.

But the moments of mentorship that stick with me are the nonverbal lessons. I know to keep cash in my wallet because I've seen you give all the cash you had to a person in need. I know how to carry myself humbly but confidently in rooms where doubters may be present because I've seen you do it.

I know how to identify and teach others how to use their gifts and talents in a collaborative setting because you've done it with us. So yes, part of mentorship is intentional but the unintentional mentorship also plays a role in teaching valuable lessons."

Jaiondra Harvey,
god daughter, Attending Oakland Community College, Youth &
Young Adult Ministry Assistant

"The journey of life is about growth thru life experiences and the journey that I have watch you take prepared you for the many roads on which life has taken you. Sometimes we believe that it's certain people, certain situations, or certain things that we must encounter for our journey to feel completed. But I believe that New Edition said it best, "Growing up can be a pain. You're not a man until you come of age," and it's in the journey. So, watching your journey from a Boy to a Man, a Man to a Father, and a Father to a Minister of God's word, it was in the journey that brought you to write this book.

Life's assignments are a part of what God has ordained in all of our lives, and that goes for the lives you have touched, are touching, and will touch. It's in the way you have played the role of father in the lives of children without a father, as well as how you have been a father to your own. But it's a part of the journey and all can see the blessings, victories, and greatness unfold in the lives of those you have impacted.

Becoming a young father, you took what was deposited in you and you gave it to Jasmine, Justin, Buster, Christian, and so many others. You were able to share the good stories and the bad stories that were a part of your journey to enhance the lives of others. All in all, it was all a part of God's assignment. I told you several years ago that you were my assignment from God, and there were things that I had to say to help guide you. I don't think that I done too bad. I remember the Saturday before your trial sermon. I had you come to the house to have the talk of how your life was going to transition for you, you listened, and let God use you in great ways.

If someone were to look at your resume, they will be able to see the accomplishments of your journey which have brought you this far. It doesn't show the pain that you had to fight through, the silent tears that you have shed, the prayers you have prayed, the victories and the defeats. But when I look at the journey all I can say is "But God".

I know that the Grandstand in the Heavens is smiling down on you, as you get ready to publish your first book. To be honest, they are not surprised because of what was deposited in you. I pray that you continue to follow God's assignment on your life. I'm proud of your journey, proud of your accomplishments, and proud of the way that you are letting God use you. Much Love, Chuckii Montgomery."

Charles "Chuckii," "C-NYCE" Montgomery,
My Favorite Cousin, Bachelors Graduate of Detroit College of
Business, Member of Kappa Alpha Psi Fraternity, Inc.

"I am eighteen years old. Pastor DJ has been much more than just a mentor; he's been a father figure, a friend, a best friend, and a brother to so many. He's been someone that would always be there whenever I needed him. Outside of church he was someone I could trust; someone I could come talk to about any problem or just if I needed to vent. He was always there with open arms and a solution to help fix whatever was wrong. When he would speak, it was so cool, so smooth I admired it. I admire the way he dresses and how he carries himself. He showed me and not only me how a true man is supposed to be and act, but also how you should treat a lady and everything he did was connected to God, Jesus Christ.

He showed me it was okay to go to church and worship and praise the Lord. He showed me how to pray and talk to God and have a relationship with him. I will never forget the things he's taught me and the things that I've learned from him. I will never forget the love he's shown me. I'm thankful for the prayers he's prayed over me, and the conversations we've had. Whether it was face-to-face or over the phone any time of day. Dad, I will cherish every moment and memory we have had and will have together. I love you more than you would ever know and I want to say thank you for all that you have done for me and my family because with your encouraging words your wisdom and your act of kindness it brought me through so many hard times and bad days more than you know. So, thank you Dad."

Joshua Owens,
Former Youth I Pastored, Attending Oakland Community
College, Graduate of Waterford Mott High School

"A mentor, by definition, is an experienced and trusted adviser. Pastor DJ has been just that and more; mentor in every area and many stages of my life. Starting from middle school, going into my now twenties, I have found myself reaching out to him to advise on steps to take to ensure success. A parent's advice is always appreciated but it means so much more when someone that is not your blood, takes genuine interest in your life's success.

I was recently in a training session on my job, and the subject of that training was Influence. We were instructed to write down our five most trusted people, outside of our immediate family. In less than 30 seconds, he was the first person that came to mind. Without a doubt, nearly ever minor/major move I have made, I have made it a mission to consult with him. I'm forever grateful that he is in my life, and... not just for a season but also for the long haul."

Tyler Rucker,
god daughter, Bachelors Graduate of the University of Michigan,
International Youth Ministry Admin

"The delicate balance of mentoring is not creating them in your own image, but giving them the opportunity to create themselves." *-Steven Spielberg*

Chapter 7

Defying the Odds

¹⁹ For though I be free from all men, yet have I made myself servant unto all, that I might gain the more. ²⁰ And unto the Jews I became as a Jew, that I might gain the Jews; to them that are under the law, as under the law, that I might gain them that are under the law; ²¹ To them that are without law, as without law, (being not without law to God, but under the law to Christ,) that I might gain them that are without law. ²² To the weak became I as weak, that I might gain the weak: I am made all things to all men, that I might by all means save some. ²³ᵇ And this I do for the gospel's sake.

(1 Corinthians 9:19-23b, KJV)

This is more than my favorite passage of scripture. It is the foundation on which I've built my ministry and relationship strategy for the past twenty plus years. Stepping into people's space to understand things from their perspective has been essential in all levels of my life's success.

As a **Son**, I learned how to honor both "My Biological" (in his elected absence) and my mother.

> [1]Children, obey your parents in the Lord: for this is right. [2]Honour thy father and mother; which is the first commandment with promise;
> **(Ephesians 6:1-2, KJV)**

I learned that the way I treat my parents, determines how long I live. So I have never, and will never, defame my biological father's character. My mother demanded respect for him of me. So I have always complied. And even in her death, I will honor the expectation that she placed on me.

> [3]That it may be well with thee, and thou mayest live long on the earth.
> **(Ephesians 6:3, KJV)**

I learned there were multiple levels of rejection and poverty. However, I grew thick skin in the process and learned that I could never quit or give up.

As a **Man**, I've learned that life isn't fair but that I don't have time to throw a pity party. I learned that it's not the test you face, but your response to the test that makes all the difference.

> **"Test of A Man"**
> **By: Unknown**
> The test of a man is the fight that he makes,
> The grit that he daily shows;
> The way he stands upon his feet,
> And takes life's numerous bumps and blows.

A coward can smile when there's naught to fear.
And nothing his progress bars,
But it takes a man to stand and cheer,
While the other fellow stars.

It isn't the victory after all
But the fight that a Brother makes.
A man when driven against the wall, still stands erect and takes
the blows of fate.
With his head held high,
bleeding and bruised and pale,
Is the man who will win and fate defied,
For he isn't afraid to fail.

The process I experienced on the path to becoming a member of Alpha Phi Alpha Fraternity, Inc., and preparing to enter the House of Alpha, brought all of my life's experiences into a focused way of thinking through poems like this one. The message here is clear, concise, and inspirational for those that pay attention long enough to see it.

As a **Father**, I learned that there was no manual and that mistakes are a part of life. However, it's not the mistake that prevents you from being successful, it's your failure to learn from said mistakes that can be your downfall. I learned that parents can create a mental and emotional tug-a-war between themselves and their children without intending to do so and that the damage from such a battle can be long lasting and detrimental to a child's development and into their adulthood.

As a **Mentor**, I've learned not to expect me from people. I'm the only me there is, but my characteristics and standards can be beneficial to whomever wants to put them into practice in their own lives. I learned that a mentor must be given permission to guide, teach to navigate, and discipline. Yet, being given this role in a person's life can be a slippery slope depending on the state of mind of both the mentor and the mentee.

I lived through the aforementioned phases of life while not fully succumbing to the preset statistical demises of black men. Yes, I became a father at twenty years of age, yes it was out of wedlock, and it was irresponsible at that age, but I have never regretted my children. I wasn't given a head start in this race called life. Most people where I'm from weren't. However, my shortcomings have been mostly my doing and I own every one of them! That being said, I still defied the odds!

> "Nothing succeeds like success."
> *-Alexandre Dumas*

I Made My Own Statistics

I've never been arrested and graduated high school at 17. I started college right away, but had to drop out. With only a high school diploma, I have worked on programs funded and supported by the Charles Stewart Mott Foundation, The Ruth Mott Foundation, Career Alliance/Michigan Works!, Action Management, The Community Foundation of Greater Flint, and the Department of Labor. Likewise, I worked for the Flint Urban League (National Urban League Affiliate), Flint STRIVE, and The Greater Flint Health Coalition.

I went back to college at the age of 38, obtained my first post-secondary degree at the age of 40, and would complete a total of three degrees in a seven-year period. I hold an Associates of Arts Degree and Bachelor of Science Degree in Leadership & Ministry from Grace Bible College, and a Master's Degree of Arts in Ministry from Grace Christian University. I've recently settled on my doctoral degree and the school where I will obtain it. I am a proud member of Alpha Phi Alpha Fraternity, Incorporated. Alpha Phi Alpha, loved by me dearly art thou!

I have made industry presentations to fortune 500 companies, presented at national educational conferences for colleges and universities, participated in policy and funding conversations with State Senators and program development with the United States Department of Labor. I have met with and participated in press conferences with the United States Secretary of Housing and Urban Development, Mayors and dignitaries from several major cities, and I have had the privilege of delivering God's word in front of thousands and in three different countries, and I continue to be advised by several Bishops in the Lord's Church. All of this is because of God's Grace and Favor on my life.

God's Plan

Today, I serve as the Next Generation Pastor of the Montgomery Community Church in Cincinnati, OH, where I am responsible for the spiritual development and pastoral care of everyone from babies through young adults. I regularly counsel parents, grandparents, guardians, as well as students from grade school to college. I serve the Full Gospel Baptist Church Fellowship International as the General Overseer of Children and Youth. It has been one of the joys of my life to help "change a generation" and I am excited to help the fellowship continue to SHIFT to the next plateau of cutting-edge Kingdom work.

In my more than 22 years of mentoring children, youth, and young adults from 6 – 34 years of age, I have always strived to make disciples for Christ through teaching, preaching, and living the word of God. Over this time, more than 300 young people have graduated high school, with many of them already having earned a bachelor's degree, many having earned masters, and 2 having earned doctoral degrees. In addition, many of them have enlisted and served honorably in the armed forces and many have completed skilled trades programs and received industry recognized credentials and certifications.

It's Still My Name

I carry the surname of a bloodline that did not want me, after being denied by the bloodline I was born to. This is a harsh reality but a reality nonetheless. I considered changing my name to my mother's maiden name after I graduated High School but I chose to keep it the same as my mom's. Now, every degree and certification has the Jamerson name one it. Every Board of Directors and Board of Advisors I've ever set upon carries the Jamerson name in its history. God has allowed me to accomplish things that this surname is now known in certain circles across the United States and other countries. Likewise, all things considered, I believe that I am the father I am today due to the absence of "My Biological". No, that does not dissolve him of the responsibilities that he should have owned up to, but I am an exception to the proverbial rule that young black men cannot succeed if they do not have a father in the home. I'm evidence that is not a matter of fact! I am not a statistic! God has always had purpose for me; of this I am sure and have no doubt!

> "For I know the thoughts that I think toward you, saith the Lord, thoughts of peace, and not of evil, to give you an expected end.
> **(Jeremiah 29:11, KJV)**

In some ways, I'm thankful "My Biological" chose not to be responsible. I've often shared that his absence motivated me to make sure my children never knew what that felt like. Because of how I had to grow up without him, I'm stronger, I'm more focused and I'm proud of myself for having persevered and conquered all that was before me. I made it with God being my helper and guide, in spite of my mistakes. I have been lied on but it backfired on the liars. Yes, I have had struggles and setbacks; some caused by my own hand, and some not. But God has always been faithful to me and those connected to me, whether they deserved it or not. Those that have been adversarial, beware, not as a threat from me, but as a promise from the Father.

"Then said he unto the disciples, It is impossible but that offences
will come: but woe unto him, through whom
they come" **(Luke 17:1, KJV)**

"But thus saith the Lord, Even the captives of the mighty shall be
taken away, and the prey of the terrible shall be delivered: for I will
contend with him that contendeth with thee, and I will save thy
children."
(Isaiah 49:25, KJV)

God has anointed me for the purpose of His Kingdom, giving me gifts to
reach people that no one else has and in ways no one else can. It is because
of these gifts alone that I have been successful thus far, and the anointing on
my life will help me accomplish everything that remains before me. It just so
happens that He chose me to do it as a "Fatherless Father."

I'm going to keep using my gifts to the best of my ability to fulfill my
purpose. I want to leave you with two statements I love to share:

"Remember that you may be the only Jesus some people may ever
see, so do your best to reflect and resemble Him well!"
And…
"If it's not yet good, Gods not done working!"

"having then gifts differing according to the grace that is given to us,
let us use them" **(Romans 12:6, NIV)**

It is in, and with this grace, that I desire to walk each and every day.

Blessings,

Thank You

TO MY WIFE:

Shawnta (CoCo) – You showed up at a time I felt I didn't deserve to be loved. My recent past had mishandled me greatly. My manhood, spirit-man, and self-worth had been demeaned and put down. I wasn't looking for you, and was actually avoiding the thought of any relationship at the time. Then you prayed. And the rest is history. Love you always.

TO MY BROTHER:

Willie Joe Jamerson, Jr. (Jay Jay) – I would not have wanted another brother to grow up with. You went through all of this with me! You held me down the entire time. We would fight because mom always left me in charge, but we loved each other through it all! You are a brilliant and gifted dude. I know it's been hard for you since mom's been gone. We will never get over her being gone, but I pray God to give you the strength you need to live with her absence. I miss her too bro! Remember, we didn't lose her, because we know where she is. Now we have to put in the work down here so we can be with her again. Man, I love you more than words can say, and may your best days of your past be the worst days of your future. You'll forever be my baby bro. #BetterIsComing

TO MY FAVORITE COUSIN:

Charles "Chuckii" Montgomery (C-NYCE) – Man, there is not enough space in my reflections to fully convey how you've impacted my life. Though we are pretty close in age, you've been more of a father figure for me than you know. I always tell you what you've meant to me during my life, so none of this is new to you but I wanted to put it in writing for the world to see. Likewise, my mom (momma

D – as you called her) loved you like a son! It was no secret how she loved you. When she transitioned to be with the Lord, I called Jay, then I called you! Thank you for being an amazing example of a son, grandson, and father! I will love and support you until I'm extinct!

TO MY CHILDREN:

I love you all so very much and I'm honored to be your father. Thank you for being the best of me.

Jasmine (Princess) – You are my most ambitious child! Only your level of determination will dictate your ability to meet your goals. May your ambitions and your dreams collide and produce the destiny you desire. My Princess Jasmine, always.

Justin (Rudy) – You are my most spontaneous child! Your dreams are huge and are only matched by your heart for your family and friends. I pray your dreams become reality and that you enjoy all that your mind, hands, and hard work produce! You've got this son. Let God lead you and there will be no limit to what you accomplish! My Prince Justin, always.

Dartanyan (Buster) – You are my most mellow and laid-back child! You are not moved by much, but your mind is sharp and your heart is as big as your 6'1" 260-pound frame! May your dreams and your heart's desires align with God's will for your life, and you experience all He has for you. My Prince Dartanyan, always.

Jarielle (Red) – You are my most emotional child! You care so deeply and love everyone so hard! You are the definition of "Rider". Thank you for letting me step in to be your dad when you needed one the most! My prayer is that God let you experience that same unconditional love and loyalty all the days of your life. My Princess Jari, always.

Christian (Bud) – You are my most spiritual child! To see you rise early in the morning to pray during your prayer watch has been one of the joys of my life! My prayer is that God guard your heart and make your spirit all the more bold so you can carry out your purpose! My Prince Christian, always.

TO MY GOD CHILDREN:

I am honored to be your godfather. You are each special to me in your own way, and I love that we all have our unique relationship. I continue to pray that God keep you and meet you in the pursuit of your dreams and goals! He will do it! Just continue to keep Him first in all you do. I love you all. Continue to be great!

Kiana Brown (BB) – You already know! Our relationship began because you tagged along with CeCe. But soon it was it's own thing. I get you! Nuff said… ☺ You have honored me so, and I'll forever be your cheerleader! My prayer is that you achieve every dream you've ever dreamt! I'm so very proud of you and can't wait to see your next. You're just getting warmed up, and I'm excited to be in the V.I.P. section!

Deandre Chilton, Jr. (The Quiet One) – Before you were born your parents asked me to be your godfather. I answered YES immediately. Your father is my brother and I've loved watching him father you. He and I are cut from the same cloth. I'm in your corner until I'm extinct son. Never forget that. I'm excited to see your future. It's already bright!

Alvin (Stephanie) Claybrooks, II. (Chop Munster/Vinyl Crookz) – Your talents are amazing son. You haven't even scratched the surface! I'm always praying for your success! You and Steph are amazing together! I pray for your union always! Remember, it is

YOUR marriage and only your voices should be the loudest. All others are just white noise. Stay focused. Your best has already been released to you. Possess it, own it, walk in it!

Arrielle Claybrooks (Legs) – My military model! You're my quiet storm. Always alert, don't miss a thing, and you hate when your family is not handled well. Sidney has always had the temper, but (to the people in the back) let it be known that you are the one that no one should make angry. IJS. Keep reaching for the stars "legs," you've got this.

Sidney Claybrooks (My Armorbearer) – Man, how do I sum up what you mean to me? I can't! But I can confidently say that watching you grow from that 9-year-old sangin' kid I met in 2006/2007, to becoming my armor bearer as a teen, to the man and father you have become and are becoming, I'm beyond proud of you. You are greater than you can even imagine. Stay locked in, keep God in the forefront, and watch Him keep working.

Deandre Elerson (The Oldest) – The godchild I tried to protect the most. The son I nearly went to jail for. It's no one's business why! We know! Your mom and granny know! I could not love you more if you had my blood Dre! I'm beyond proud of you. I charge you as the oldest, as the leader, as the first, to never quit believing God. Never! He can do everything you need Him to do. You just have to continue to ask, and continue to believe!

Jaiondra Harvey (My Sneaker Girl) – I've told you this before, but I'm telling you where the world can see, "You Did Not Fail!" Now pause and thank God that He allowed you to hit reset. He's got you right where He wants you. Be faithful, be focused, and I know you'll be great! In fact, you're already great. Thank you for trusting me to be a voice in your life. Love you real big.

Jaice Harvey (Babygirl) – My butterfly! You have gone through such a metamorphosis since we came into one another's lives more than 16 years ago. You and Arri are the goons (referenced with love ☺) of the god kid bunch. I have to make sure you guys are far away from the naysayers, so you don't lay hands on people. In all seriousness, you have blossomed into an amazing young lady and it's only up from here. Stay focused and stay authentically you! It's the only way to live. I'm proud of you. Don't stop, don't quit.

Dash DeVaughn Jefferson (Dasho) – The first of your name! The protector of Declan, Dream, and Baby Los! The Best big brother ever! Man, I love you so very much! I'm proud to be your godfather. Keep being great and watch God's plans for you continue to be revealed. You've got this! My Guy!

Declan Darnell Jefferson (Decco) – My Linebacker! They're not ready! Can't wait to see you do your thing! Now go find your shoe because I'm sure you're missing one at this very moment ☺

William Henry Murphy, IV (Quatro/4) – You are my most misunderstood godchild. But I get you in ways many don't. I do not count it lightly that you honor me as your godfather. Remember God is faithful and it's not our fight. You just keep clean hands, a pure heart, and stay focused. STAY TRUE TO YOURSELF. It's all up from here!

Tristian Patton (Dude) – The way you love your mom and family is amazing for your age. I'm proud of the student and athlete you've become. I pray that God blesses you greatly and that you achieve every dream. Don't focus on who's not in your life, rather focus on who is! Stay in God's Will son. Go get it!

Tyler Rucker (YF) – You are my most resilient godchild. So much of your upbringing mirrored mine. Being the oldest child in the home, having the responsibility before you should have, and having to figure it out most times on your own. You've already won love! The devil couldn't take your mind, he couldn't break your spirit, and he couldn't make you quit! You win! I'm beyond proud of you, and I will be riding with you until I'm extinct. Be Great Ty!

Brandon Robinson (The Nascar Kid) – Hey B. I know so much has happened in the first few years of your life. But you are a ray of sunshine to your mom and the rest of the family. Your heart is so big and I'm honored to be your godfather. I promise I'll tell you a lot of funny stories from when your mom and me were growing up. I know she made a funny face when she read that last sentence. LOL. I'm so proud of the respectful kid you already are, and am excited about your future. Love you B.

References

The Bible (King James, The Message, and NASB translations)

Jakes, T.D. (1997). So You Call Yourself A Man? A Devotional for Ordinary Men With Extraordinary Potential. Tulsa, Oklahoma: Albury Publishing

Quotes from:

Alexandre Dumas

Mahatma Gandhi

Stephen Spielberg

Sean Stephenson

CPSIA information can be obtained
at www.ICGtesting.com
Printed in the USA
BVHW050804080522
636222BV00053B/1077